Networking for Business Development

A Guide for Attorneys and Consultants
By Bruce D. Sunstein

IDEAS FOR LEADERS
CHANGING THE WAY WE THINK

Publisher's Note

Every possible effort has been made to ensure that the information contained in this book is accurate at the time of going to press, and the publishers and authors cannot accept responsibility for any errors or omissions, however caused.

No responsibility for loss or damage occasioned to any person acting, or refraining from action, as a result of the material in this publication can be accepted by the editor, the publisher, or the author.

First edition published in the United Kingdom in 2024 by Ideas for Leaders Publishing, a business of IEDP Ideas for Leaders Ltd.

Apart from any fair dealing for the purposes of research or private study, or criticism or review, as permitted under the Copyright, Design and Patents Act 1988, this publication may only be reproduced, stored or transmitted, in any form or by any means, with the prior permission in writing of the publishers. Enquiries concerning reproduction should be sent to the publishers at the following address:

Ideas for Leaders Publishing
42 Moray Place
Edinburgh
EH3 6BT
www.ideasforleaders.com
info@ideasforleaders.com

ISBN
978-1-915529-40-4 – Hardback
978-1-915529-41-1 – E-book

*To my wife Ann, whose love, character,
and brilliance continue to inspire me, and to my
partners, for their support of the tenets underlying this book.*

Table of Contents

Introduction

In this guide. I share what I have learned about business development over the last four decades since founding my law firm, where I still practice law. You, my audience for this book, may be a lawyer in "our firm" – the firm where I work – or you may be a lawyer elsewhere, or you may not be a lawyer at all, but a consultant keen on selling your services or your company's services in a field outside of the law. Regardless of which of these situations fits you, the effort and attitude required are similar – so, welcome!

Paradoxically, achieving success in business development does not generally come by asking someone you know (whom we will call "your contact") for business. Instead, success comes by creating, in your interactions with your contact, a context in which your contact will feel comfortable to entrust you with business, and, at some propitious moment, actually take the plunge to give some business to you. In this guide, I focus on how to establish that context.

Creating a context in which your contact feels comfortable in entrusting you with business requires cultivating a winning mindset. Greet your contacts, whether new or established, with assurance, genuine interest in their affairs, and enthusiasm for their efforts. A greeting like this inspires confidence. How do you find new relationships or maintain your established ones? In this guide we focus on how you can grow your network and develop that winning mindset to enhance your opportunities for business development.

Not all business opportunities arrive with a label "NEW OPPORTUNITY." Part of business development is to be alert to recognize when a potential opportunity has arrived, and to find a way to capitalize on it. For example, if a colleague needs help on a project, and you judge that the prospect for downstream business is remote, you might still offer to help, because you sense that your gesture of assistance would be well received. After a short while, your colleague might ask you to run with the whole project. Making such a gesture to collaborate would then have produced an internally driven business opportunity for you, one that will deepen your network and your reputation.

As this example illustrates, opportunities for business development can sometimes be enhanced, if not created. Finding and seizing an opportunity for business requires your personal attention and will reflect your personal style. There is no single best path for business development, because on every path you can find a potential for new business, and the path you take will inevitably reflect your personal style.

Your opportunities for landing business are enhanced, not only by a winning mindset and a good list of contacts, but also by embracing and projecting the culture of your firm and its core values. Your firm's culture becomes evident to potential clients as you interact with them.

In your firm, one of these core values stands out in particular— respect. Respect is having due regard for others' feelings, wishes, and rights. Respect is most clearly manifested in relationships with others: respect for colleagues, respect for supporting personnel, respect for clients and potential clients, respect for judges and administrators, respect for opposing counsel. There is a reflexive aspect as well – self-respect, namely, having due regard for your own feelings, wishes, and rights.

While the core value of respect, like the ground on which we walk, provides support for relationships with clients and colleagues, those relationships gain direction from another of one of the core values: passionate focus on clients.

Respect and passion for clients' creativity and achievements guide client interactions on a daily basis, by inspiring heightened attention to their legal affairs as well as efforts of the firm to make a difference for them in their lives.

Respect involves a long-term focus on what is essential to a durable relationship: what does the client need? How can you, as a trusted advisor, be helpful to your client? How does your client prefer to hear from you? By what steps can you provide your client with the most powerful representation and how might you most effectively involve your client in formulation and carrying out of these steps? How can you make your client's experience of your representation both productive and transformational?

Respect is a core value because it sparks other related behaviors:

- Listening well to understand the individual's affairs and challenges, from the individual's point of view
- Being curious about the individual's needs, ideas, and aspirations
- Showing generosity and compassion toward the individual and a willingness to help the individual in achieving the goals that matter most to the individual
- Following up with the individual over time to keep the relationship fresh
- Persisting in development of a relationship with the individual

These values—listening well to the individual, being curious about the individual, showing generosity toward the individual, following up with the individual over time, and persisting in developing a relationship with the individual—are behaviors that are fostered by respect. Each of these values is the subject of one of the following chapters of this guide.

Implicit in these values are showing and sharing enjoyment of the client relationship with your client. Although money is a part of your relationship with the client – you work with the expectation of being paid – what propels the relationship is not the money but rather your collaboration with the client in addressing your client's legal or other needs. That collaboration works best with how you show and share your enjoyment of your relationship with the client.

Although it is easy enough to understand the importance of values to a law firm and law practice, it is a different matter altogether to internalize and manifest those values in your professional life – to make them part of who you are. Attempts at faking a professed adherence to values may quickly be discovered by the very individuals whom you are most seeking to impress. It is essential to use your self-awareness to assess regularly whether you are reflecting your values in your relationships with your clients and what you might do to enhance these relationships.

In showing respect imbued with passion for your client's enterprise, while coupling insight and advocacy in your lawyering, you have a good shot at bringing into your network all sorts of contacts, including advisors, referral sources, potential clients, and actual clients, and at having some great collaborations downstream with colleagues and clients.

Please read on to learn how.

CHAPTER 1

Solidify
and Expand
Your Network

Networking for business development is an art, and the foundation of that art is your professional network of individuals, regardless of how you happened to have developed it thus far. The goal of this art is to deepen existing relationships and to grow new ones, so that you are the one who first comes to mind when a need for a trusted advisor is in prospect. As you embark on business development, the question is less about where you are in the development of your network, than about how you are going to further develop it. This chapter provides you with some tools and practices to advance your business development repertoire. Adopting the mindset and practices presented here will contribute to your success in business development and to making your firm a dynamic place where lawyers, staff, and clients are satisfied and engaged, and where your client base is continually growing.

Because your professional network is the community of people with whom you meet and connect, your network needs your consistent, personal touch to make you memorable and to maintain its growth. The individuals in your network must be the object of your active engagement. Make an effort to keep them informed about your professional activities and remember to express interest in theirs.

Your potential clients, and your peers, need to know who you are, how to find you, and what you do, because a potential client will not engage you in a vacuum.

The potential clients whom you most desire need a context in which it makes sense to engage you. Your network, properly developed, provides that context, so that you will inspire confidence and provide your potential clients with a rationale for engaging you. The broader your network, the more likely it is to produce a good response on your behalf for a prospective client vetting your qualifications. The more you cultivate the relationships with the people in your network, the better they will know you, and the easier it will be for peers and potential clients to find you, trust you, recommend you, and for clients to hire you.

The basis for growing your network is a great contact list, and a great contact list is more than just names; it is made up of people who know you, know what you do, can say something positive about you, and will pick up the phone when you call. Business development takes time, especially at the beginning of your career. When you commit yourself to **building your network** and **working your network** every day, it will become part of who you are and how you practice. Clients will seek you out more often and know where to find you.

Seven Essentials for Building Your Network

1. Develop your list of contacts.

To build a contact list, you need tools. Software changes rapidly and not every firm uses the same tools. Make sure you learn about what Customer Relationship Management ("CRM") software is in use in your firm and how to use it.

At your firm, the first tool, and simplest, of tools might well be the Outlook contact manager. Another related and essential tool, which can be synchronized with Outlook, is InterAction. Whereas Outlook conveniently tracks all your contacts, InterAction conveniently lets you and your colleagues track all contacts that have been shared among colleagues of your firm. It is preferable to enter all new contacts directly in InterAction. Learn how Outlook and InterAction work.[1]

---

1 Open it in Chrome or MS Edge. Adding your new contacts directly to InterAction avoids duplicate entries and informs you of others in the firm who know the contact. However, it is possible to use Outlook for first entry of your contact. To do so, you must specifically change, for that contact, the field in Outlook called "Contact State" to require that your contact is "Shared with Firm." Otherwise, no one else will know about your contact.

2. Organize your list into tiers.

Because your list of contacts will grow over time, it is valuable to develop immediately a list of categories that can be used in these tools to identify types of people in your network. For example, your categories may include neighbor, alumnus of your college, alumnus of your law school, client, potential client, attorney, source of funding, etc. These categories are easy to add to Outlook and will show up in InterAction as well. Additionally, Outlook and InterAction have a field called "Notes," which you can use to enter specifics of where you met the contact, and things you want to remember about the contact. If you are working with your assistant or a colleague on this project, you can, in an e-mail, specify your categories and your Notes for that contact.

3. Schedule a regular block of time weekly for working your list.

Your network is not merely a list of contacts. It is a living and dynamic set of relationships. It is important to stay in touch, at least with your most important contacts, and you cannot expect to do so by meeting them on a random fashion. Therefore, an essential part of maintaining a network includes meeting with

Develop a habit of meeting with a different person each week who is, or whom you want to be, in your network. Planning time to meet with your contacts is essential.

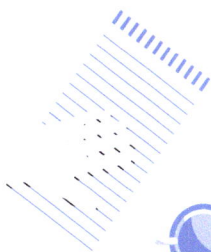

people who are in it and people whom you would like to add to it. Develop a habit of meeting once a week (preferably in person, otherwise via Zoom or Teams) with a different person each week who is, or whom you want to be, in your network. Planning time to meet with your contacts is essential.

4. Meet. Once you have a meeting scheduled with your prospect, invest in the meeting.

This is your opportunity to connect with your contact and to show your contact that you are interested in and care about your contact's activities. Consider going to meetings where you would enjoy meeting the participants and where you can prospect for meeting others to add to your network. If once per week seems too audacious, then choose a frequency you can achieve. Even if you meet a potential client or referral source once a month, over time that will make a difference. If you are meeting someone whom you do not know well, do some research on this person ahead of your meeting. Focus your conversations with your contacts on their needs and interests and on how you might be able to help them.

5. Keep track and follow-up.

Preferably, your network development activities can be planned rather than arbitrary actions. Good networking requires goals and discipline, so keep track (for example in a spreadsheet) of individuals whom you have met or are planning to meet, and lay plans to follow up! Find reasons to reach out to your contacts on noteworthy occasions for them or for you.

6. Promote yourself.

Your tool kit for tracking contacts should be expanded to include one or more social networks. LinkedIn has maintained itself as a professional-only platform, whereas other social networks, such as Facebook, Twitter, Instagram, and TikTok are used by some for professional and personal networking. Make good use of social media. As you connect with people in such media, add them to InterAction or your firm's preferred CRM system. Whatever platform you use, drive your contacts into your professional network through connections and put their information into the firm's system. You can collaborate in identifying, pitching, and signing potential clients in your CRM system. And vice versa: consider inviting individuals whom you have added to Outlook/InterAction to connect with you in LinkedIn, etc. – but only individuals whom you want the world to know are in your network. LinkedIn can keep you apprised of career moves by your contacts. Over the long term, you must find ways to promote yourself and your firm. Do not hide your light under a bushel basket! Post messages to your contacts on LinkedIn. Write articles and get them published. Give presentations.

7. Enjoy yourself.

Think about the person you want to be and how you want to be remembered when you meet with others. Think about the people you have recently met and the impressions they have made on you. Are you more likely to refer to the tense and grumpy person, or to the accessible and cordial person? Know yourself and bring your best self to every meeting.

Attending professional networking events can be an excellent way of expanding your network. Professional networking events do not have to be sources of anxiety if you keep your eye on the purpose of the event and develop a repeatable approach. Take a moment to pause mindfully before you enter a networking event. Take a breath. What would success look like? How can you gamify the event; set a goal so you can succeed?

What do you have to do to walk away with at least two names for you to follow-up with after the event? Did you previously identify a guest of interest who will also be present? What do you have to do to meet that person and set-up a follow-up meeting? In short, develop an objective, repeatable approach to initiate encounters at networking events and even informal gatherings.

As you do these things to build your network, you can deepen your relationships with your contacts by developing your skills in interacting with them as discussed below.

CHAPTER 2.

Listen Actively

Maya Angelou said this: "I've learned that people will forget what you said, people will forget what you did, but people will never forget how you made them feel."

Developing your network involves more than accumulating names you have listed in Customer Relationship Management software, and more than meeting with your contacts. The "more" includes *active listening* because, without active listening, meetings with your contacts, including prospective and current clients, are less likely to be valuable or memorable for them or for you.

Active listening, inspired by the core value of respect, requires having and showing authentic curiosity, interest in, and empathy for your contact's affairs and challenges. When you demonstrate interest in this way, you have shown that your contact's experiences matter to you. Your interest and empathy are invitations to your contact to invest in the relationship with you, as a result of being heard, understood, and respected. Showing interest and empathy to your contact requires another attribute, self-awareness. You cannot project these things to your contact unless you develop self-awareness and use it in your relationship with your contact.

Active listening includes learning to manage potentially awkward silences in discussions with your contact. Silence can often arise when conversation takes a serious turn or when something said needs time to sink in to be fully processed. Allowing silence to linger provides a gift of time to dwell in that moment. It is important to learn how to be comfortable with managing silences because emotions are contagious. When you are mindful, you are better able to maintain calm for longer during a period of silence. Awkward silences can occur when either party to the conversation feels uneasy for any reason, and the uneasiness envelops the interaction. You must find a way to return to neutral to provide time and space for your contact to open up at a comfortable pace about the challenging situation. One way to help is by breaking the silence with a question, "And what else is important for me to know about xyz?"

My first experience in earnestly facing silence was in Quaker meetings. A Quaker meeting often involves sitting in prolonged silences, while waiting to hear something. It takes practice, steadiness, and confidence to sit for a time in silence without feeling it is your responsibility to fill the silence. Similarly in meeting with your contacts. Pauses in conversations are often no more than the result of natural ebbs and flows of dialogue. Some pauses are longer than others. Develop the confidence to sit with your contact in silence, during which time you can concentrate on what has already been said. Consider that when you take it upon yourself to fill the silence, you might be doing it for the sake of your own comfort or because you have assumed that others are uncomfortable.

"Wait, what?" you may be thinking, "I want to learn about marketing, but you are talking about listening! Isn't marketing about selling and selling about talking, not about listening." Isn't that correct?

In fact, it is not correct. Marketing is more about listening than it is about talking. In this respect, marketing involves the practice of active listening. Listening is an art, and an art that requires heart, discipline, and time. Listening involves more than allowing the words to reach your ears. Hearing is only the beginning of listening. Something must happen after the words have reached your ears!

Or, to put it another way: if you are talking, you are not listening. When you are talking, your mind is identifying thoughts of relevance that you are passing on to your listener. When you are talking, your mind is shaping those thoughts and converting those thoughts into speech that can be heard by your contact. It is a common tendency to succumb to the sound of one's own voice, especially in an apparent moment of brilliance. If you find you are dominating the conversation, remember the acronym **W.A.I.T** – *Why Am I Talking?* Is what you are saying in service of providing value for your contact? If you are not sure, then stop talking and start listening.

I offer the heretical proposition that listening requires effort. And, in fact, listening well requires practice along with some self-confidence, and it requires *comfort in dealing with silence*. Your contact needs enough room in a conversation to say things to you that might be hard to say or – at times – hard for you to hear. Give your contact room to say it and yourself room to hear it. Cultivate calmness in order to stay focused on the client's objective rather than on the challenging feelings that come up in the course of a difficult conversation.

Make silence your friend. When you are in a difficult negotiation, for example, you should ask the question or make your point, and then – this is the hard part – you must wait. Allow silence to do its work. Allow your contact to have an opportunity to respond. If you are filling the silence that would otherwise be used by your contact to respond, you are missing an opportunity to connect with your contact and depriving your contact of the opportunity to feel heard and understood by you.

Business development involves cultivating trust and inspiring potential clients to invest in a relationship with your firm. In marketing interactions, your contact will communicate ideas, needs, and aspirations, while you typically seek to demonstrate that you appreciate these things and that your firm can provide support to address them. In these interactions, you can be more successful when you practice active listening, using these five steps.

1. Step One.

Ask open-ended questions that invite the contact to tell you what is going on.

2. Step Two.

Listen without interruption to provide your contact with an ample opportunity to speak. Do not assume pauses are the time for you to respond. Watch your contact's body language and ask whether your contact has completed sharing their thoughts and whether you can respond. By allowing for the presence of silence in the conversation, you will learn about and follow your client's communication pace and style, providing a reception that will contribute to ease of communication and lay the foundation for trust to grow.

3. Step Three.

Process the words your contact has shared with a view to understanding what those words mean to your contact. You should develop a methodology for careful listening. As a part of that methodology, you should develop the skill to uncover for yourself what truly matters to your contact. Consider:

- What overt and underlying messages is your contact sending?
- Why is your contact choosing these precise words?
- Is your contact reciting things objectively and rationally or is there some underlying, and more complex, unarticulated concern?

You will be perceived as respectful – not dense – if you ask, *"let me make sure I understand what you said.... (Paraphrase)."* If you get it right, the contact will feel heard and understood. If you are a bit off the mark, then you will appear confident to the contact when you openly acknowledge the correction and continue to give your contact the gift of your attention and focus.

4. Step Four.

Engage in conversation with your contact. When you converse with your contact, *look your contact in the eye* to show your engagement. In carrying out *active* listening, when you engage in conversation with your contact, make your engagement in conversation responsive – *but not dominant.* An effective way to engage is by asking WHAT questions, answers to which reveal more about how the contact feels or thinks about X. WHAT questions elicit more information about your contact's experience from their point of view. Asking open-ended questions invites the contact to elaborate, shows your interest in learning more, elicits key information about what matters most to your contact, helps you determine whether the contact would be a good client for your firm, and builds trust. Asking great questions provides an opportunity to develop an understanding of what is important to your contact so you can home in on the value that you could provide.

Where appropriate, you can ask open-ended questions that show you have been thinking about strategic aspects of your contact's experiences:

- What is it about X that matters to you?
- What is it that is most challenging for you about X?

- What approaches have you considered as a way of addressing your concerns about X?
- What options are still available?
- If you were to take approach Y, what would be your concerns and what would you like about that approach? What would be an ideal out-come?

Become accustomed to asking open questions, and your success in meeting new contacts will melt away your discomfort, as you play the game of building your professional network.

5. Step Five.

Develop and deliver an appropriate response to your contact. The most appropriate response is not necessarily the response that directly addresses the greatest needs of your contact. It is rather the response that shows you have been listening closely, you care, you can identify with your contact's circumstances, and you stand ready to do what is right in the context. Resist the urge to editorialize. Resist the urge to problem-solve. From having asked your WHAT questions in step (4), you have heard your contact tell you what matters most. Figure out a response that shows you have correctly understood what your contact has told you, before you offer any opinions or advice. "Thank you for helping me understand" is a good way to get started with your response.

The strategic objective of any meeting is to develop a new client or a good referral source. Active listening is one of several skills to help you get there. Aim to display these qualities:

(a) Presence: Demonstrate that you are paying attention to your contact.

(b) Empathy: Provide meaningful responses to and questions about your contact's experience of living under the described circumstances.

(c) Self-Awareness: Facilitate and manage your own interaction with your contact.

(d) Confidence: Build trust by speaking with confidence about what you know and asking questions about what you do not know.

(e) Preparation: To facilitate conversations with your contact, do homework on your contact in advance of the meeting to learn details about the person's work environment, special interests, and publicly available personal information, etc. Develop a list of things ahead of time to ask about to deepen your understanding of your contact and what professional challenges your contact may be facing.

(f) Follow-up: After your meeting, keep in touch with your contact. Reframe the meeting as just the beginning of an on-going conversation.

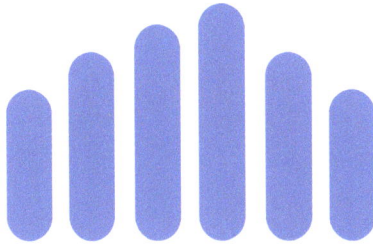

Listening well requires practice along with some self-confidence, and it requires comfort in dealing with silence.

CHAPTER 3

Be Curious

You cannot develop business with a business prospect until you have first earned your prospect's trust. "Earning the trust of a stranger sounds impossible," you might say. You are correct. Although you cannot earn the trust of a stranger, you can convert that stranger into a contact who knows you by demonstrating your curiosity about who the contact is, what your contact needs, and how you can best serve your contact.[1]

"OK," you say. "How do I demonstrate my curiosity?" You need to find things out about this contact and show this contact that these things matter to you. "How do I find out things about this person?" you ask.

Asking questions provides you with a path forward, and asking questions of your contact is a way of demonstrating the core value of showing respect for your contact. In demonstrating respect by asking questions, you can also project your passionate focus on your client's concerns and your drive to combine technological insights with skilled advocacy to provide a strategic advantage.

---

1 There is an important exception to the principle that a stranger cannot instantly become your client. If you have inspired trust and confidence in a referral source, your referral source may inspire confidence in someone whom you do not know to hire you.

What Matters Most?

Designing questions is a skill you can develop. As you get to know your contact, the questions you ask will likely depend on your contact's specialization and focus, since those are the things that will likely structure your relations as a consultant or attorney with your contact. For example, in marketing my services as a patent attorney, I typically provide a session that I call "Try before you buy." The potential client is invited to a 90-minute session, for which we do not charge. In this session we talk about the client's invention, and I seek to develop, within that same 90-minute period, at least one patent claim and definitions of some of the important terms used in the claim. I bring this up, because, in such a session, the potential client asks me what I want to know about the invention. My answer is almost invariably: "Tell me what matters most."

"What matters most?" is an open-ended question that leads to a major discussion of the technology, along with the contact's interests and passions. Asking questions allows you to structure the conversation around how the contact sees the world and how your contact would like things to be different. Indeed you can ask any of your contacts to tell you what

It is OK to ask the same questions and to tell the same story in front of successive individuals.

matters most. Expanding on the points we discussed in Chapter 2, on active listening, practice asking – "What" and "How" questions:

- What do you think about X?
- What is important about the technology?
- Why is it important to you? Your company?
- What led you to the discovery?
- How would the technology impact the current way of doing things?
- What reactions have you experienced to X?
- What do you think is the biggest obstacle?
- To what related contexts might the invention also apply?
- What areas look ripe to competitors?
- What constraints in these related contexts would enhance or detract from the opportunity in these contexts?
- And what else?

It is OK to ask the same questions and to tell the same story in front of successive individuals.

As a further example, work as an intellectual property attorney frequently involves representing inventors and companies hiring inventors. The skilled IP attorney makes a point of following the development path of the invention. One of the hallmarks of an invention is non-obviousness. The inventor's development path therefore frequently involves attempting to do what everybody else would have thought at the time was a bad idea. Your questions can explore this path: "What led you to try doing something that everybody else knew [of course they were wrong in thinking this] was a bad idea or even stupid?" You can with relish and enthusiasm uncover a story, usually buried, about the surprising thinking that led to the invention. Your questions show your appreciation of the inventive process and can lead to deeper insights into the invention and its relation to the "*prior art" (the way of doing things before the invention was made). Each question will lead to another as you uncover the story, and these questions will show your passion for your contact and for the invention.

Besides uncovering a great story, your questions can explore potential expansion of the inventive ideas. Are there related contexts to which the invention might also apply? Are there constraints in these related contexts that would enhance or detract from the opportunity in these contexts?

Also, all the questions that you have for your contact could be questions already being explored by competitors in connection with their own activities. In other words, questions that you are directing to your contact may well be questions that you can direct to others in order to get a valuable perspective. You can ask of your contact what areas look ripe to competitors – starting with your contact's own implementations, but also branching into other potential implementations. Questions along these lines can show your empathy for your client, and they can also show your strategic thinking – because the answers to such questions may well lead to a point of view of the invention that had not been apparent to your contact, as well as to patenting things that had not been in the front of the mind of your contact. In such a case you have developed additional business even while working on existing business.

Although your contact may well be the inventor whose inventions you are seeking to patent, you can ask similar questions of expert witnesses and other witnesses in litigation where patent infringement is at stake. There is a symmetry here: you can also ask similar questions of the other side – of expert and other witnesses in litigation where patent infringement is being asserted *against* the party on whose behalf the witness will be testifying. The answers will probably

Respond to what the contact says, not to what you are thinking that, in your opinion, might be more brilliant or insightful than what your contact has said.

be different, owing to the different point of view of the witness, but your approach to asking questions will be similar in each setting and your questions can provide answers that will broaden your perspective on your contact.

We have pointed out that business development requires a winning mindset and an actively growing and deepening network. Another important quality we

touched on in the previous chapter is self-awareness. Your questions can better project interest in and empathy for your contact when you have a heightened sense of the impact your contact's responses have had directly on you.

"Now that I have asked a question, what comes next?" Listen to your contact's response to become informed about what matters to your contact. Allow what is said to lead you to your next question.

As we learned in Chapter 2, what is involved is not merely hearing. Respond to what the contact says, not to what you are thinking that, in your opinion, might be more brilliant or insightful than what your contact has said. At the very least, transition to your comment by acknowledging what your contact has said.

By asking questions and listening to the answers, you can focus on learning about your contact and about your contact's needs, ideas, and aspirations. Accordingly, you can convert a stranger – such as the person you meet at a networking event – into a valuable contact by asking thoughtful, open-ended questions that demonstrate active listening and your focus on this person's needs, ideas, and aspirations. When engaging with a contact, project your winning mindset of assurance, genuine interest in your contact's affairs, and enthusiasm for your contact's efforts. Intentionally project curiosity and empathy in your contact's affairs. Remember to use the tools we have discussed previously. Enter your contact in your Customer Relationship Management software (such as Outlook or InterAction), categorize your contact in it, enter in "Notes" some things to remember about your contact. And follow up with your contact.

CHAPTER 4

Be Generous

In the movie *Miracle on 34th Street*, a Macy's employee named Kris Kringle, in recommending, to a Macy's department store customer, that the article of the customer's interest could be found in Gimbel's department store, inspired the head of Macy's to make it a Macy's policy to refer customers to the competitor when Macy's did not have the item in stock. Gimbel's followed suit.

One has the sense that Macy's and Gimbel's businesses thrived with this policy. Indeed, generosity of this type makes great business sense. A business book, *The Go-Giver*, by Bob Burg and John David Mann, advises us to think first, not about what we can get from a contact, but rather what we can do for the contact.

It may sound backward, but in fact it is conventional thinking that is backward. You can develop business only when you provide value to your contact. Working in this way is important because you need to provide a compelling reason why your contact should spend time with you and trust you. In a relationship with your contact, you need to find ways of demonstrating a willingness to assist your contact in achieving things of interest to your contact. Think like a dandelion, not like a cashier. Throw your generosity to the wind and it will bear fruit in its own time where it finds fertile ground. The art of networking is not transactional. If you give with the expectation of receiving something specific within a specified amount of time, you will feel frustrated and deprived. Trust the process. Relationships and referrals take time.

Demonstrating this willingness is not a matter of doing a lot of work without compensation or allowing your contact to take advantage of you, but rather a matter of making meaningful gestures that show your empathy, competence, and confidence that you can assist your client in achieving your client's goals.

In sum, meaningful networking gestures involve *sharing* – sharing your time, sharing your insights and empathy for the client, and sharing your enjoyment of working with the client. Sharing enjoyment is a form of generosity–namely emotional generosity. When your client sees that you are actually having a good time in performing services for the client, you are showing the client that your collaboration with the client matters to you and is fun. Your joy, reflected in the client's experience, can show the client how your guidance can make an emotional difference as well as a legal difference.

The authors of the *Go-Giver* emphasize that

a business must focus on delivering value to the customer, preferably exceeding the customer's expectations. A lawyer or consultant must similarly focus on delivering value by one means or another to potential and current clients. Your current clients, if you please them, will be a source of referrals and return business. In that respect, every current client is also a potential client and a potential referral source.

Sometimes the giving shows up in surprising ways. One of my firm's partners in prosecuting a patent application for a sports product for a client of many years figured out that he could get a patent, based on the client's pending application, that would cover a product made by a competitor. When the competitor initiated patent infringement litigation against my firm's client, the client was able to sue the competitor for patent infringement and to put the competitor on the defensive! The creativity of my firm's partner provided a welcome and unanticipated benefit to the client by casting the client as the injured party and the competitor as the infringer.

If that were not enough, the partner performed this same trick a second time with a different client and a different competitor. What matters in this context, however, is not that the partner was brilliant–which

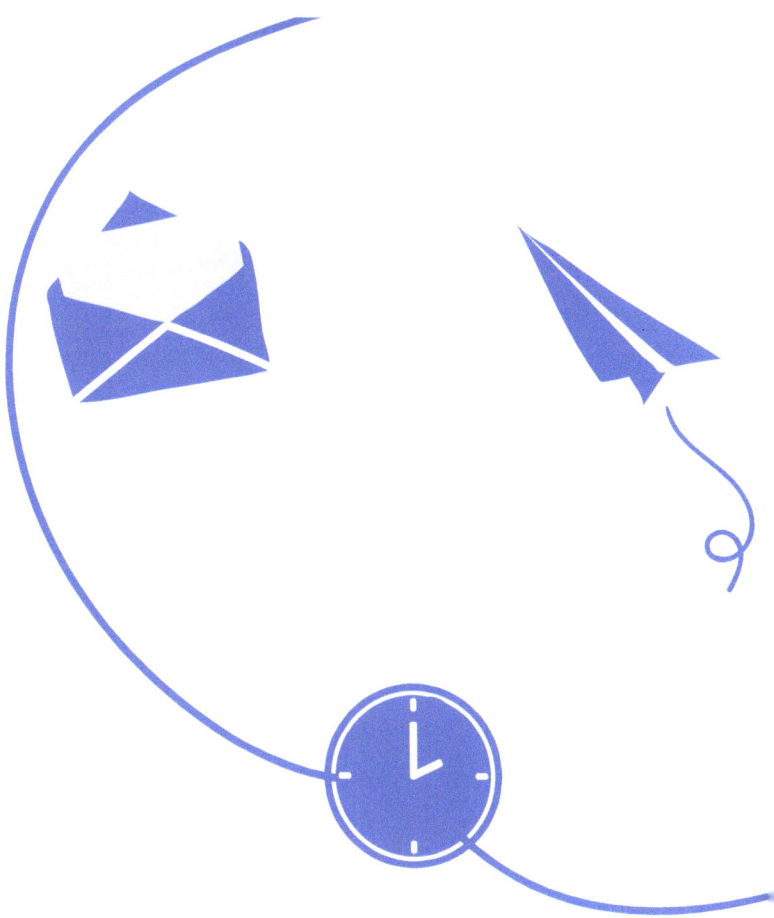

To use a network well it is important not to keep score. Instead focus on what you can do for your contact, and the results will be more likely to accrue to your benefit.

he was–but that his performance for his contact exceeded expectations in every respect, providing extraordinary value to the client.

You can also show generosity by sharing with your contact one or more individuals in your network. If your contact happens to be seeking an accountant, for example, and you know an excellent accountant in your network, you can share your information about the accountant with your contact. In this way, you earn points with your accountant in the network for making the referral, and you have harnessed the power of your network to confer a benefit on your contact. Be alert for opportunities in which you can benefit your contact by sharing individuals in your network.

But what if the accountant in your network should meet your contact and determine that your contact is a dud – someone who is not good client material? You do not want the accountant to lose confidence in your referrals. You need to be proactive. At the time you make the referral, tell the accountant (if it is true) that you just met your contact, and that the accountant should review independently whether your contact is good client material. A wise referral to another professional in your network should be

66

Be yourself, everyone else is already taken

Oscar Wilde

sufficiently nuanced to allow the professional to make an independent professional judgment about the person being referred.

To use a network well it is important *not* to keep score. Instead focus on what you can do for your contact, and the results will be more likely to accrue to your benefit. The *Go-Giver* suggests that "most of the time, what people call 'win-win' is really just a disguised way of keeping track." The book points out that a focus on "who owes who what, that's not being a friend. That's being a creditor." If you are sharing some information or advice with your contact, it is to your benefit to feel rewarded by the act of your sharing rather than by receiving something in return from your contact. That selflessness is likely to be recognized by your contact and enhances the prospect that your contact will engage your services downstream. The flip side to feeling rewarded by the act of your sharing (rather than by receiving something in return from your contact) is to remain open to opportunities, including those surprising ones that arise when you least expect them. You have doubtless met individuals who seem gifted at being lucky. But luck does not usually reflect random conditions. You can increase your chances of a favorable outcome by entertaining opportunities to transform the present set of circumstances into success, for example, by connecting a person in your network with another

person in your network. The old saying that "it is better to give than to receive" misses the business point. While it may indeed be better to give than to receive, it is better yet to remain open to receiving when you are in the course of giving. Be alert to opportunities to grow your business from your relations with contacts in your network.

Another point to keep in mind is that you must demonstrate genuine interest in your contact. If you cannot show real interest in your contact, skip it. You cannot fake interest in your contact. You have to mean it and to show it. If you find yourself unable to focus on and engage with your contact, then ask yourself, "what is it about this conversation, or this person, that is leaving me uninspired and uninterested?" It is possible that the prospect might not be a good one for you. Listen to your instincts. If you cannot engage well with a contact, try to understand why, and then decide whether to try again, or to refer the contact to someone else, or simply to let things go and to move on.

Be yourself; everyone else is already taken. – Oscar Wilde

At bottom, these insights mean that is essential to develop qualities and networking skills that make you a valuable part of your network, a trusted advisor who is able to share with, as well as receive from, individuals in your network. When you focus on what value you can give to your contacts, your contacts are more likely to think about how to reciprocate. Networks are a kind of mutual aid society where your own opportunity can come in the course of your giving. The market-savvy attorney knows how to give and take selflessly and not get distracted by keeping score. When Kris Kringle demonstrated generosity, he was also showing Macy's and Gimbel's how generosity can be good for business.

CHAPTER 5

Follow Up

Accumulating contacts is a big achievement for the attorney or consultant seeking to develop business, but it is not enough merely to have contacts. These contacts must be converted to active, dynamic, sustainable relationships in your network.

Subject to some rare exceptions, if you are waiting for any given one of your contacts to get in touch with you out of the blue, the odds are that you will not be contacted. If you are hoping that luck will put you in touch with one of your contacts, you will need to find ways of making your own luck. Following up with your contacts is essential to increasing your chances of getting known and getting business. You have complete control over whom you will reach out to and no control over whether someone will return a call or reach out to you. Focus on what you can control and do it well.

Following up does not mean pestering, and intelligently following-up requires you to be sensitive to concerns of your prospect. Trust your instincts if you start to feel you may be intruding or annoying. On the other hand, before you reach out, do not assume that you will be annoying. As long as you remain respectful and open, the phone works both ways. You can hear from a contact if you have made it easy for your contact to get in touch with you.

If you are waiting for any given one of your contacts to get in touch with you out of the blue, the odds are that you will not be contacted.

More generally, it is important to follow up with contacts because, without follow-up, relationships tend to become stale. Even without losing the contacts, the contacts will not think of you in time of need; the goal is to be front-of-mind when someone is thinking about needs in your legal field.

Have an actionable plan. Following up should include a plan with a list of goals and a method for achieving them. In short, you need an *actionable plan*, as opposed to random, *ad hoc* acts of marketing.

Arrange your contacts in tiers for follow up. Not all contacts are created equal. Your plan needs to take into account the fact that some contacts are more promising than others. You should consider having a tiered list of contacts with whom you would seek to be in touch directly. One tier might involve contacts you have met while doing work with clients. Another tier might involve contacts who are classmates from college. Another tier might involve contacts from law school who have careers in law. It might be your plan to seek to connect via phone or Zoom with one contact in one of the tiers every week, and rotate through the tiers in successive weeks. For example, I have made a special project of cultivating contacts who are involved in funding companies or who are investing on their own account.

Your plan for follow-up needs to address the *processes* of how you select your contacts for follow-up, what communication medium you will use, as well as the *timing* and frequency of your efforts.

Not every follow-up needs to be initiated the same way, and in fact, often a particular occasion will spark a particular type of follow-up. One does not have to have an excuse to follow up, because there are many different ways and reasons to follow up. Arguably overthinking this can reduce the quantity and quality of follow-ups, especially for those of us who worry about how a call might be received. For example, if you have been out of touch with a key contact for several months and want to reconnect, you can make any of these gestures by e-mail:

1. Send a friendly "Hi, you crossed my mind..." email;
2. Send an article with a note;
3. Forward to your contact a relevant business opportunity;
4. Think of someone who may be of interest to your contact and ask whether your contact would like an introduction; or
5. Prepare a specific e-mail to a specific individual on a particular occasion, such as a promotion, an external event having a bearing on the contact,

such as a program in which the contact has participated, a work anniversary, or an award given to the contact.

Using social networks can increase your leverage in following up. You can comment on a LinkedIn post and post it so that it goes to all your LinkedIn contacts. Instead of sending a specific e-mail to a specific individual about one of the particular occasions listed just above, you might be able use that occasion as a basis for a LinkedIn post about your contact that you can share with all of your LinkedIn contacts. Or you might have seen a third-party post or an article that has a bearing on your contact, in which case you can share it with your contact via e-mail with a comment. And, sometimes, a follow-up includes asking your contact for information or advice.

Find ways to engage your contact. In following up with contact, you should focus on approaches to your contact that are engaging. By way of contrast, it is not engaging to spend time with your contact talking only about yourself.

In a similar vein, consider a LinkedIn comment that you have posted to all of your contacts. What is good about such a post is that it can be seen by all of your contacts. But that is also what is bad about

Following-up involves developing and enhancing relationships, and doing so requires responding to events, communications, and circumstances in a way that engages your contact

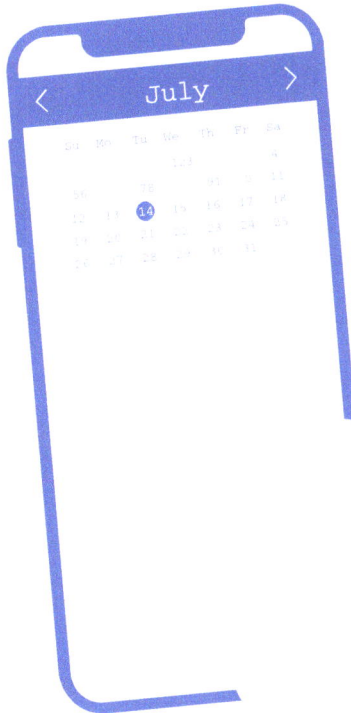

71

such a post! It is bad because it is not directed to a specific contact, and it does not require a reaction from a specific contact. The most powerful follow-up involves a back-and-forth series of communications, so that a relationship is further developed. In the long run, following up involves developing and enhancing relationships, and doing so requires responding to events, communications, and circumstances in a way that engages your contact. Ideally, you interact in a way that shows your involvement in things that matter to clients.

Because time is precious and limited, it is fine if some of your follow-up involves posts to LinkedIn, for example, rather than e-mails to specific individuals. Preferably, these posts should be leavened with more focused communications where there is some back-and-forth.

Keep track of your efforts. To follow up requires discipline. It is a good idea to develop a reminder system. It is possible to use InterAction or another CRM to set up reminders that are linked to a specific contact. For your contacts who are in the investing space, for example, you can use a spreadsheet to track your activities.

At bottom, your efforts in following up should be

directed to activities that might remind your contact to think of you in time of need.

As one fortunate example, I have kept in touch over several decades with a business manager with an MIT technical background, whom I have known since the days when he worked with a well-known inventor who was a client of my firm for many years. From those days, my business manager friend knows a talented mechanical engineer, who worked with the inventor and started a medical device company. The engineer needed some patent counsel, and my business manager friend recently advised the engineer to contact me. The engineer did so, and now I have the medical device company as a client. That was great luck, but also due at least in part to efforts at my end that reminded my business manager friend that I exist. Over time, your own efforts can work in a similar manner.

Work on following up with your contacts with regularity and focus. Good luck!

CHAPTER 6

Persist

Negative responses to your efforts in building your network and in seeking business are unavoidable. You must learn not to take personally these negative responses or silences. Every person seeking to develop business is on a unique professional journey, and finding the right clients and referral sources takes patience, persistence, optimism, and self-awareness. If you treat prospects and colleagues with respect and make the most of every opportunity when you interact, then you can feel good about your efforts regardless of the outcome. Why do people who love to fish return happy and determined to try again even when they catch nothing? The collateral benefits of engaging in the activity are inherently gratifying and will, if nothing else, build skills that will increase the likelihood of success next time.

Building your network requires deferring your gratification. You cannot expect immediate success in developing business when you seek to meet with a contact. Furthermore, do not expect to receive an "atta-girl" or "atta-boy" for taking networking risks associated with promoting yourself. Develop a technique about which you feel good, and the reinforcement will come when you get a referral or sign a new client. Some people whom you meet will be

Every person seeking
to develop business is on a unique
professional journey, and finding
the right clients and referral
sources takes patience, persistence,
optimism, and self-awareness.

neither a suitable client nor, in some cases, a contact suitable for being in your network. Sometimes it is a wiser course to let go of a questionable contact or a questionable prospect.

Everyone seeking to develop business has a fear that a contact will not respond in a desired manner. Dealing successfully with that fear by acknowledging it and normalizing it will enable you to build your network more rapidly and effectively. What are some of the things you might be telling yourself ahead of time about why a contact might not respond as you would like?

- "Won't like me."
- "Not interested in getting my advice."
- "Thinks I'm calling to sell and doesn't want to pay my rates."
- "Has other priorities now."

Although any of these fears may later be supported by the turn of events, it is equally possible that they will not be. Maintaining your mindset matters in this context. Consider that the worst possible outcome of your encounter is simply the message that the recipient of your invitation will turn it down. Notice when your inner voice holds you back from your efforts to connect. Take a chance and respond to receiving a "no" with as much gratitude and confidence as you would if you get a "yes."

The purpose of your network building is not to have your contact like you, but rather to have your contact know who you are, know what you are doing, and respect your professional competence. To maintain a positive mindset, you must acknowledge your inner critic who shows up with negative messages about your worth and what you are offering. There is no way of knowing what the other person might be thinking. To regain your confidence, it is essential to return to active listening – focusing on the needs of your contact – and to trust the process.

Remember who you are: an experienced and capable professional who can render services at the highest level. You would not have been hired by your firm if you were otherwise!

Another way in which you can address your fear of rejection by a contact is to consider that meeting with a contact involves a two-way street. Yes, you want your contact to appreciate being in your network, but simultaneously you must also evaluate whether you want your contact to be in your network.

The double-sided nature of the interview. In this same vein, consultants to the legal profession remind attorneys that it is essential to *qualify* a contact as a suitable prospective client. Would the contact be an appropriate client for you and your firm? That is the principle that comes into play at this juncture.

In other words, one of the challenges in business development is figuring out whether a prospect would make a good client! The fact that some prospects do not make good clients is not, however, a reason to stop trying to show your prospect that you care about the prospect.

You must keep in mind that, although not all prospects are good ones, all prospects can become good referral sources. Therefore, in general, do not write off a prospect.

What three qualities make a prospect a good one? (1) The prospect must prize quality and not be a bottom feeder, looking for the lowest possible price. (2) The prospect should be sophisticated and able to appreciate a professional with nuanced judgment, who addresses the risks and rewards of a range of possible actions. (3) The prospect must be able to handle the truth. (4) The prospect must be financially secure and able to pay your bills.

Here is a story, about dealing with a contact, that illustrates the ambiguities and possibilities that permeate business development. A few

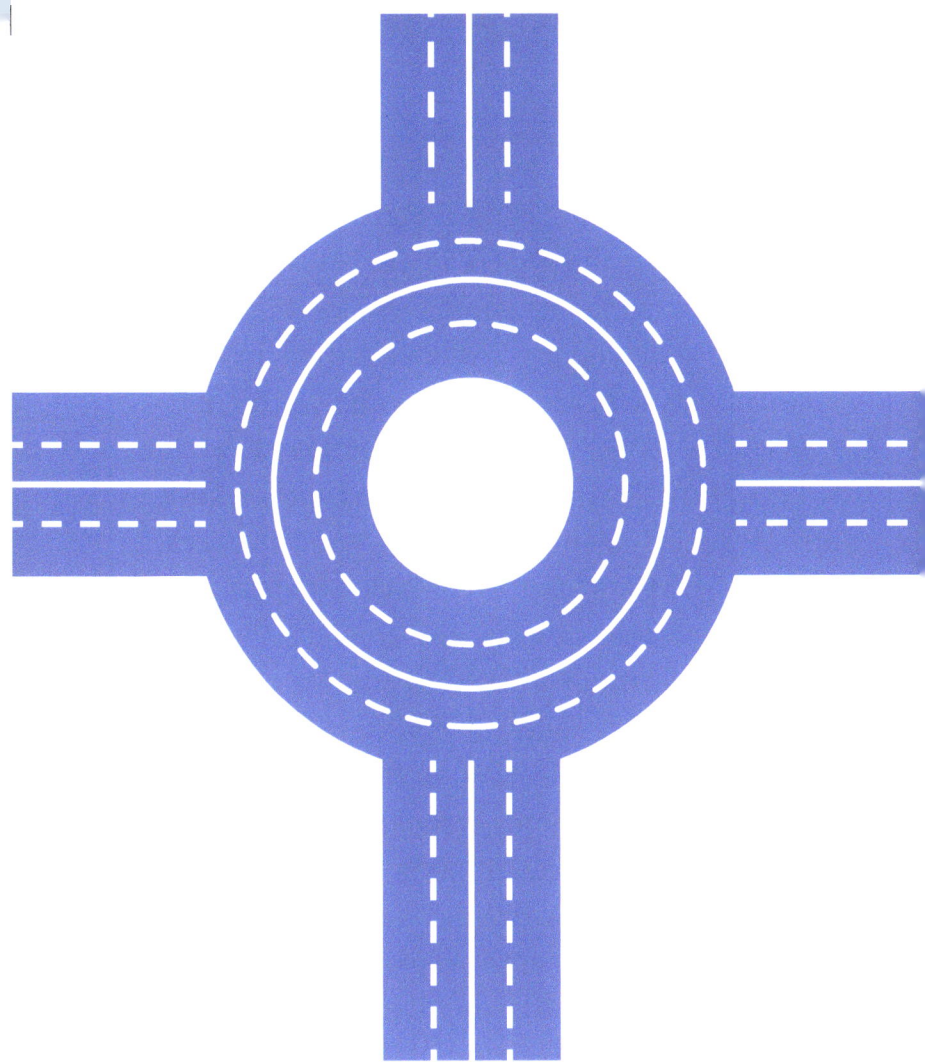

Although not all prospects are
good ones, all prospects can
become good referral sources;
do not write off a prospect

years ago, I was advising a start-up company, involving two brilliant MIT PhDs. After my work with the company was going forward, one of the PhDs left the company and later started another company, which is concerned with medical data processing. Apparently remembering a good time working with me, she called me seeking advice about patents. A routine conflict check revealed that we had a conflict with another client. A partner advised me that the conflict was waivable, and I worked to prepare a waiver agreement. Eventually, I determined that to effectuate the waiver would require my PhD contact to disclose some information to a third party, which happened to be my existing client. Because my PhD contact did not want to make that disclosure, we lost the representation.

At that juncture, however, I had more to do in order to turn square corners. After investigation of the options going forward, I referred my PhD contact to three outside patent attorneys in whom my firm has confidence. And I wrote to each of the three patent attorneys to tell them that I had provided their name to my PhD contact as one of three attorneys who could provide representation to her company. By coincidence thereafter, she asked me about some advice she received from yet another attorney, and I told her that the other attorney was mistaken, and I explained why. In responding to her, I did find the occasion to mention that if she should happen to become comfortable with making the disclosure to the third party involved in the waiver, then we could put the waiver in place and I could represent her.

Although I had not expected this turn of events to lead to business directly with her company, later my PhD contact did engage me and my firm to work for her company. In the meantime, each of three other patent attorneys has been informed that they were recommended to my PhD contact for possible representation. In this manner an experience that began with disappointment was transformed into a success by persistence over time.

In this connection, you might have an experience with a contact that fails to net you an enthusiastic response, or perhaps any response at all. Don't let the lack of a favorable response get in the way of pursuing the contact. Sometimes a non-answer is not the same as a "no." Your contact might say yes to something else. When one reaches out to another person, one

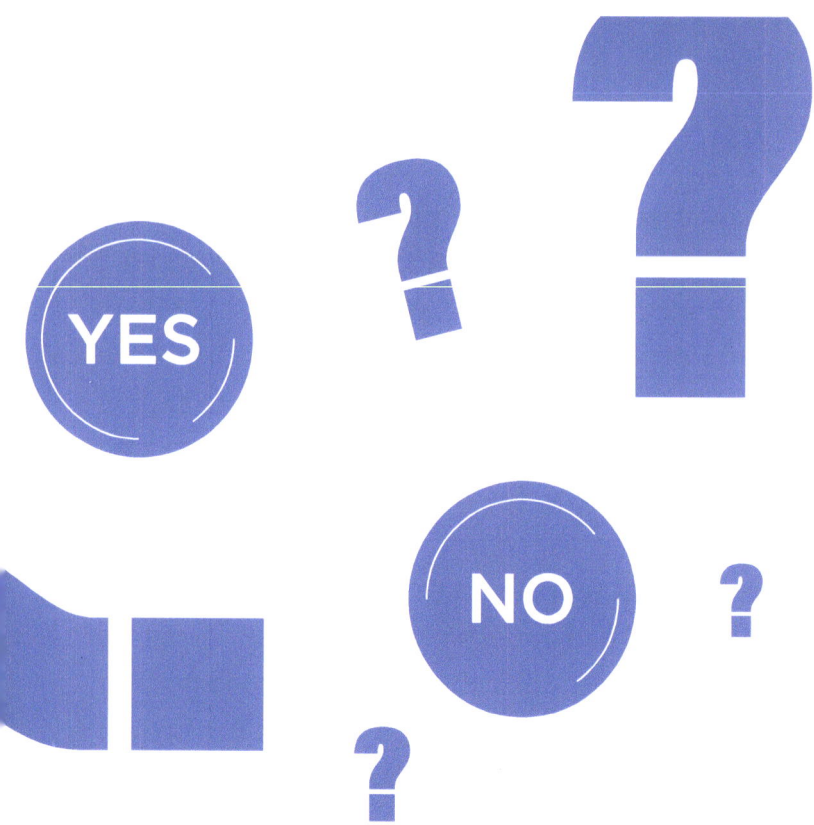

Notice when your inner voice holds you back from your efforts to connect. Take a chance and respond to receiving a "no" with as much gratitude and confidence as you would if you get a "yes."

cannot know what that person is going through at the time. Therefore, patience and persistence matter. In fact, after a failed attempt to land a client through a contact, one of my partners maintained communications with the contact for well more than a decade and a number of job changes by the contact, with the eventual outcome of not just one, but several, great client referrals from the contact.

Seven steps. From reading this pamphlet, you can discern seven steps of a business development practice:

1. Develop your contact list.
2. Organize that list into tiers – college classmates, law school classmates, work acquaintances, etc.
3. Schedule a regular block of time weekly for working the list.
4. Select prospects to contact, contact them, and get them in your weekly schedule.
5. Do your research before you meet with someone whom you do not know well.
6. Interact with your prospects, focus the conversations on their needs and interests and on how you might be able to help them.
7. Track your progress through the list and follow up.

As to item six, there is a whole gamut of types of interaction to consider:

(a) in-person meetings (breakfast, lunch, coffee);

(b) video meetings;

(c) telephone conferences;

(d) e-mail exchanges and chat in LinkedIn;

(e) LinkedIn postings (one-way); and

(f) newsletters.

You can see that I have listed these types of interaction in an order proceeding from the most intimate encounter to the most impersonal experience. In general, you can correctly imagine that the more personal the encounter, the better it is. The challenge for the busy practitioner is that the more personal the encounter is, the more time it requires. On the other hand, investing the time required for a personal encounter may well be more likely to produce a favorable result.

Landing the big client. Although sometimes there can be surprises in your opportunities, do not expect to land a big client immediately. Over time, your law school classmates and college classmates will have positions of responsibility and can give you business. You must develop habits to facilitate getting referrals out of this network. To nurture this network is typically a matter of investment over years, not minutes.

What if your persistence indeed provides you with a chance to land a big fish as a client? Note that sometimes a firm's attribution rules will provide origination credit to the person whose contact is most responsible for bringing in the client. Asking another professional in the firm to assist you in bringing in the client does not need to cost you attribution credit. But if you are asking the other professional to do a lot of work, for example, doing investigation or preparing a presentation, then maybe you would want to share the credit.

Spillover effects. Your activities in business development are not conducted in a vacuum. You can see that many traits that are important in marketing are also important to the rest of your law or consulting practice, and, indeed, to the rest of life: active listening, comfort with silence in conversation, being generous, following up, and persisting. Over time you will experience the full force of your efforts. What you do well now in business development is related directly to what will emerge for you during the rest of your professional life. May you prosper in it!

CHAPTER 7

Navigating the Arc of the Client Relationship

Your network includes not only contacts whom you have met but also your clients.

And your reputation with your clients, which will affect your ability to develop business in the long term. will depend on how you perform in serving them. For these reasons, you should consider how you and your colleagues address the entire arc of the client relationship, which is the focus of this chapter.

You cannot take new clients and current clients for granted, because client relationships are necessarily in a state of flux. Lawyers or other professionals in a firm should demonstrate warmth and interest to all at every stage, lest an opportunity to retain or secure a client be passed over. Similarly, it is important to pay attention to the client relationship, to anticipate shifts in client needs and circumstances.

The arrival of a new client – and of a new matter for an existing client – marks the beginning of a new relationship, and that relationship must be cultivated in order for it to flourish. Although the firm's role is to address its client's legal or other problems, the firm's relationship with its client is personal. Clients care about how they feel when they are interacting with the firm's professionals, and they want assurance that their trust in the firm is well placed and that their resources devoted to counseling and representation are well spent.

To provide clients with this assurance, you must grasp and share the risks and the big picture affecting the client. In this context, while the client will certainly identify problems it faces that must be solved, some of the problems facing your client may not be readily apparent. It is up to your firm to elucidate these problems and the context of these problems as well as to provide a perspective for action.

After these apparent and not-so-apparent problems have been identified, then you can develop a plan, a team, and a budget to address these matters. A client needs to receive status updates on a regular basis. The plan should therefore build in a schedule for communicating regularly and effectively with the client to apprise the client of what has been achieved to date, where the billing stands in relation to the budget, and what remains to be done. Although some of these status updates can be provided by e-mails, e-mails alone will not be enough, because these are delicate matters going to the heart of the firm's professional and personal relationship with your client. Where possible there should be in-person meetings, and if in-person meetings are impractical, then consider video conferences and telephone conferences.

Related to the plan, the team, and the budget is managing client expectations of costs and outcomes. From the outset it is essential to develop and deliver a clear-eyed assessment of what your firm will be charging the client, how your firm's filings will be received in the relevant forum (whether a court or government agency, etc.), and the likely result of your representation. Developing this clear-eyed assessment requires objectivity, while delivering the assessment also requires empathy for the client's circumstances. A classic example of managing expectations arises when you are representing a client in litigation. With a litigation project, normally the stakes are high and the litigation consumes extensive resources of your client. What will the client think if you lose? In many cases, a loss can be expected. You must talk with your client from the outset about the large risk of a loss and about strategic moments in the course of the litigation when outcome-determinative decisions have to be made or can be made. You must prepare your client both for success and for failure, knowing that one of these outcomes will prevail. While you can take some credit for your success, you can be sure that the client will be inclined to blame you for failure. So you must work, repeatedly over time, on shaping your client's expectations for the outcome of the litigation.

Many projects have outcomes that are more complicated than a simple loss or victory. To prepare your client for whatever objective you seek with your client, you should work with your client to frame the range of possible outcomes, while indicating that forces outside your control may prevent achievement of the objective.

Communicating with your client about a project involves more than planning for a range of potential outcomes. Billing is an important form of communicating with the client and must be understood in the context of the client relationship. Billing should be prompt, fair, and consistent with the budget. If there is a potential divergence (definitely something to be avoided), it must be addressed early, with urgent importance, and great sensitivity.

In cultivating your relationship with a client, it is important to develop a vision of what the client relationship is capable of becoming. What is the client's potential – for your firm, and for the client? That vision should be examined in the context of your vision for the firm. What kind of clients do you want and what kind of clients can you represent? Imagination is required here, because, in your firm's experience, some miniscule clients, over time, may have developed into great ones. And some clients, already substantial, may have failed to provide you with assignments on which your practice can thrive.

Therefore, in cultivating your relationship with a client, you must regularly ask yourself, what are the prospects for you in relation to this client going forward? If the things with the client are going well and the prospects going forward are good, then you should be working hard to sustain and improve the relationship. On the other hand, not every person or every business makes a good client. If the client does not want to invest in intellectual property (or the firm's particular expertise) at the level you think is appropriate or imposes unrealistic budget constraints on projects, for example, then the client is a good prospect for winnowing.

Winnowing a client should be handled with a level of attention and respect matching the level of attention and respect you provide to a new client, because (among other reasons) you do not want the client being winnowed to speak ill of you to others who may be looking for representation. As to the client being winnowed, you may, for example, work to find alternative counsel for the client and to assist the client in experiencing an orderly transition to the alternative counsel.In evaluating your client relationships and in cultivating them, you should consider that your ideal client wants services from you that you can well deliver, appreciates working with you as you deliver these services in a manner fulfilling for the client and for you, and pays you promptly. Although no client may be completely ideal, it is up to you to work to help each client move in the direction of the ideal.

What happens when your business development has been successful, and you have all the clients you think you need? You should probably think again! Keep in mind that, usually, each one of the projects on which you are currently working will reach an end. What will happen when your client's project reaches this end? Is there follow-on work? If so, what assurance do you have that your firm will get it? If there is no follow-on work, then what? Ironically, sometimes when you are busiest with work, you need to be thinking about how to replace that work when it has been completed. Business development should therefore receive your constant attention, even if it is not your full attention. The trick is to keep business development in front of mind while still carrying out the substance of the work on which your firm depends for its continued existence. Put another way, business development is as much a lifestyle as it is a source of livelihood. For this reason, you should work to find ways to make business development an interesting and pleasurable pursuit, one which you can maintain over the course of your career.

The Introduction mentions the importance of showing and sharing enjoyment of the client relationship with the client. That shared enjoyment helps to support collaboration with the client in rendering legal or consulting services. But sharing enjoyment of the client relationship produces another benefit, over the arc of the client relationship, by helping to frame your relationship to the firm's practice. In that light, your counseling or representation is not merely the providing of consulting or legal services for a fee but rather a career infused with the warmth of positive human relationships with your clients. In that context, you, and the firm, can flourish.

My deep appreciation to Beth Masterman,
President Masterman Executive Coaching, for her professional
coaching and guidance, and to Roddy Millar,
CEO of Ideas for Leaders, my publisher, for his
sagacious editorial advice.

A WORD FROM EXECUTIVE COACH, PAMELA J. GREEN

The organizations I get to work with today want to achieve their competitive advantage - outperform others in the space. Likewise, the executives I've been working with also want to achieve an advantage, one that makes them a distinctive leader. This means they are in a constant state of trying to outperform themselves and be viewed as a standout leader in their organization, their field, and their industry.

Being a distinctive leader propels you to the best opportunities available to someone with your talent. As an organization, having executives who know how to leverage their distinction means you outperform anyone who considers themselves a competitor. This is especially true today, where both the business and its leaders must have their ears to the ground to know how and when to make needed shifts to survive. To help you accomplish this, I will present you with information and scenarios to help shape your thinking and improve your analysis and problem-solving skills through real-world situations. But how?

By working toward three goals outlined for you in this playbook:

Head Goal

Intentional focus on understanding how you think and what influences that thinking is the beginning of self-awareness and thus the beginning of change. **Think:** *What am I watching? Whom am I interacting with? What am I doing that influences my way of being and my way of leading and could be preventing me from seeing different perspectives?*

Heart Goal

To influence a deeper connection between yourself and your world. You'll learn that emotional connection is what deepens our experiences and influences our behaviors. Reading and walking away without allowing even the slightest impact is an exercise in futility. **Think:** *What will I do with what I know? How will I leverage it to improve myself, my brand, and my leadership? What do I need to know to expand my worldview and remain competitive?*

Life Goal

To intentionally adopt new practices that move you to think on new levels and to behave in productive and progressive ways. **Think:** *What new skill will I challenge myself to practice? How can I improve my approach to leadership? How can I become the type of leader people want to follow, engage, and support?*

It doesn't get any more personal than addressing what is going on in your mind, your will, and your emotions. All three are responsible for the paths we've created and are critical in creating new paths that result in the development of your brand. If you really want to achieve a competitive advantage and distinguishable brand, then you'll have to create new neural pathways that open you up to new ways of thinking so you can become the person you desire most, and scenario-based learning works. Here's how to experience this book:

1. Once you complete each section, **Review** the content again to reinforce the learning. In fact, scholars suggest reading something three times to boost retention.

2. Next, sit and **Reflect**. Reflection is where the REAL work happens because self-awareness is the beginning of change. Reflection has a way of deepening the experience.

3. In your time of reflection, **Ask** yourself some of these questions:

   - What stood out for me as important?
   - What do I need to do differently or better to get improved outcomes?
   - Who do I want to become?
   - What assumptions am I making that are interfering with what's possible?
   - How will these changes help me get there?
   - What am I learning about myself?
   - What is emerging as a blind spot?
   - What's still getting in my way?
   - What am I holding on to that I need to let go of?
   - What excuses am I making?
   - What rewards do I anticipate for making needed shifts in my conduct, attitude, and behavior?

4. **Complete** the action plan by defining exactly what you'll do to make improvements. While you won't need to do this for each of the practices presented, focus in on at least one or two for the next six months. Find someone like a coach or friend to hold you accountable, and when you believe that change has been cemented, move on to the next practice.

5. **Practice** new behaviors by working through each scenario presented. Practice leaders practice new ways of thinking by challenging their assumptions and revealing what's possible. The immediate feedback from the scenario will help you learn more quickly from your decisions.

6. **Refine** yourself by freeing yourself from behaviors, ideas, and a mindset that no longer serves you. This requires you to turn off cruise control.

7. **REPEAT**. Repetition reinforces neural pathways and deepens learning.

Allow me to challenge the traditional way in which you think. Are you where you want to be, and if not, what needs to change? In this playbook and journal, I am providing you with the key practices and an easy-to-follow system for thinking like an executive brand - a brand that is cross-capable and able to make countless contributions, sometimes in different but related areas of your performance.

Extensive research proves there really is no such thing as a smart or dumb person. We all have the same brain capacity, minus medical diagnosis. The true distinction is in having focus, how we use our brains, and our willingness to do the work to rewire our thinking. The research shows that you can change your mind, and through this journal, I'll show you how. Get into the habit of reading, writing, thinking, meditating, and practicing new ways of leading. Without doing so, you run the risk of a system takeover. Yep, the glial cells in your brain might consider that unattended piece of new information (conference keynote, book, coaching session) as waste and, well, erase the message in as little as 24-48 hours.

Unlike in the sister book *Think Like a Brand*, I'm NOT going to make it easy for you because if I did, you'd think executive leadership was easy, and you and I both know it is not. You may have to dig deep in some areas to see your desired results.

REFLECTION

What's your level of readiness for real and meaningful change? Who do you think can support your desire to make significant shifts in your conduct, attitude, and behavior? What emotional experience do you want others to have from interacting with you?

....

....

....

....

....

....

EXECUTIVE MASTERY

Executive Mastery occurs when a leader excels at technical, social (people), and conceptual skills such as critical thinking, communication, creative thinking, decision-making, and analytical and abstract thinking. Researchers such as Robert L. Katz, credited with developing the skills theory, defined these three areas as developmental, ones that the leader can cultivate. As you might have experienced, the further you climb the corporate ladder, the greater demand is placed upon your social and conceptual skills than your technical skills. It could be said that your technical expertise "got you here," but your technical expertise alone is not sufficient to sustain your acceleration.

In addition to mastering your technical, social, and conceptual skills, there are two additional reasons people are not getting and keeping the careers they desire most. According to research by OI Global Partners:

67%	**64%**
They do not sufficiently differentiate themselves from others	They fail to successfully transfer past experiences to the current job opportunity

What makes you a distinctive brand?

Maintaining a growth mindset is germane to the making of a master and distinguishes you from everyone else. If you've learned how to challenge your assumptions and thinking and curate new information, then you're THINKING in new ways and ready to secure the next level of mastery.

You are considered the master of your brand when you make repeated actions that inspire the behaviors of others towards the successful achievement of personal and business goals. This requires adaptability, flexibility, and intentionality. You can't pack up all that previous experience and think you'll be able to simply unpack it in the new role or organization like clothes in a suitcase. Everyone, including you, will be disappointed. Therefore, every leader must exhibit proficiency in leading themselves, leading others, and leading the organization, and that is how this playbook and journal are organized.

Mastery affords you the ability to recognize the need to shift your thinking and communication styles to induce respect and followership.

How you think, perform, and interact with others, especially your social skills, matter and are of primary concern to boards and executive teams today. Use this playbook and journal to examine *16 crucial practices* that can lead to your executive mastery:

Phase 1:
Leading
Yourself

1. Your Thinking
2. Being Centered
3. Your Behavior
4. Accountability
5. Coaching

Phase 2:
Leading
Others

1. Leadership Styles
2. Communication
3. Conflict Leadership
4. Collaboration
5. Delegation
6. Your Network

Phase 3:
Leading the
Organization

1. Culture
2. Decision-Making
3. Meeting Practices
4. Practice Leadership
5. First Team Leadership

Mastering these areas of leadership will support your career sustainability while helping your brand and your organization remain nimble and adaptable to the ever-changing business environment.

REFLECTION

Now that you realize leadership is more than your technical ability, how would you assess your executive mastery?

THINK LIKE
A BRAND **RECAP**

I'm going to assume that you've completed the foundational work outlined in my book, *Think Like a Brand*. If you have not completed this work using the outline I've detailed in the book or another outline, then these executive-level practices might prove challenging. Here is a summary:

☐ **Get clear on your "why."** What is your "calling" in life? What is the vision you have set for yourself, realizing that it takes shape over time?

☐ **Determine your career aspiration.** Leveraging your "why," what do you want to get paid to do and to be known for? Your career aspiration is directly connected to your legacy.

☐ **Identify your non-negotiable conditions for employment.** What are your must-haves for your next opportunity or future opportunities?

☐ **Write your mission, vision, and evaluation of your values.** What will drive your decisions and keep you engaged in future work opportunities?

☐ **Create a list of your short-term and long-term goals.** Keep in mind these can and will change.

☐ **Conduct your brand research.** Will there be a demand for your talent in the coming years? How will that demand affect your earning potential? Or your desire to achieve executive-level career opportunities? What areas of your talent need fine-tuning in order for you to remain competitive?

☐ **Identify your organization's brand, needs, and priorities.** How are you aligned with your current organization? How can you create alignment to ensure long-term satisfaction? If you can't align with your current organization, what adjustments can you make in the short term while you explore your other options?

☐ **Create your executive confidence template.** Your Executive Confidence Template is how you package and present your talent daily. If you ignore, reject, or skip this step, then you have volunteered to live the life you have instead of the life you want.

☐ **Showcase executive-level credibility.** In a room or a business meeting, would you describe your brand as a church mouse or a brave eagle? Which one gets noticed and perhaps taken more seriously? Consider this as you are strategically demonstrating the executive-level competence of your brand.

☐ **Identify your brand adjacencies™.** What if you don't want to do what you're doing for the next ten years? Have you ever considered that you might want to do something different? This work will allow you to pivot when/if necessary and extend your brand in exciting ways while also leveraging your talent for adjacent career opportunities.

☐ **Strive to become principled.** Principled executives strive for excellence with high regard for what is right and wrong. They operate from a personal set of ethical standards for which they will not compromise. Is your brand trustworthy? Does your reputation carry a message of credibility and moral character?

REFLECTION

In which of these areas do you need to apply more energy and effort?

....

....

....

....

....

....

SET YOUR MIND

When my dad was 62 years old he was diagnosed with terminal lung cancer. He was a lifelong smoker and a welder by trade. My son had just been born, and we were devastated at the news. I was a daddy's girl, so the thought that there was nothing we could do overwhelmed me. He went through chemo and radiation and did everything doctors and specialists told him to do. The day he told us the news of his diagnosis, he also said, "I'm not ready to die, so please don't bury me with your tears and sadness." "What?" I thought, "I can't cry? How exactly is this supposed to work?" For him, I set my mind not to cry. Instead, I meditated on good things and focused on enjoying the time I had with him. But it's not my mindset that is the focus of this story; it's his.

Because my dad loved traveling and family events, we planned trips and did family stuff in a big way. We traveled by car, from Ohio to Florida, to Disney World that summer, our favorite family vacation spot. We did all the community festivals, and we allowed him to eat everything he wanted to eat. I swear, he is the reason KFC is still in business today. Thanksgiving and Christmas were always big family events and were not downplayed that year. We didn't pretend that his health wasn't declining; we just decided, as a family, not to give it any energy. We didn't know how great a mindset's impact could be until he passed.

You see, my dad died one and a half years after his terminal diagnosis. That's one year and three months longer than the doctor's prognosis. The doctors gave him two months to die. Instead, my dad pursued another year and three months to live. He wasn't ready to die, and he lived to prove it. That is what a mindset is.

**Set your mind ahead of time on the things
you want to happen.**

What do you want to happen with your brand and in your career? What emotional experience do you want others to have from interacting with you? You decide where you are going and how you want to get there, and I can help guide you using the following pages of this book.

Set your mind:

1 Focus on the good things you want for yourself and others.

2 Believe that every experience can be used for your good.

3 Release negative experiences so they don't permanently imprint your thinking.

4 Identify the needed change in your conduct, attitude, and behavior.

5 Say what you expect for the outcome - out loud.

6 Put what you believe into practice.

PHASE 1:
LEADING YOURSELF

1. YOUR **THINKING** MATTERS.

Case Study

"What made you this way?" is the question I found myself thinking about upon engaging a colleague. I couldn't figure out how his brain and his mouth were connected. I thought, "Does he hear himself?" and "Who did this to you?" Real brain teasers. The more experienced I became, the more I realized that there were lots of leaders like him. Leaders that simply stopped learning and instead opted to allow their brains to go weak. They might attend conferences and learning sessions, but much like going to the gym and not putting in any effort, they gain no cognitive value from the investment. The answer to "what made you this way?" is they stopped learning and growing.

A cognitive (knowledge) gap occurs when there is an increase in the availability of new information related to an area of work that the performer has not yet acknowledged, acquired, and/or applied to enhance their performance.

The world is always changing. Information travels too quickly for you to combat cognitive dissonance with constant "head in the sand" rejection of new information or anything that contradicts your beliefs about something.

To achieve advantage, executives must combat cognitive gaps by staying relevant, educating themselves to elevate their thinking. Reading, writing, researching, networking, and exposure to important topics facing your profession and the industry or organization are vital. This doesn't mean you have to stay buried in a stack of books; the entire organization must embrace knowledge management and transfer.

To combat cognitive gaps, ask yourself these types of questions:

- What is happening in the industry?
- What challenges are on the horizon that we need to be prepared for?
- What technological advances are affecting our work?
- To what extent are we or are we not equipped to respond to crisis situations?
- What types of scenarios threaten the sustainability of our business?
- Are we attracting, retaining, and rewarding a top-notch diverse pool of candidates?
- Are we future proofing our talent pool?
- Which biases are preventing me/us from seeing what's possible?
- What must we do that is unique, different, or better to remain competitive?

Each of these questions and more is being explored by organizations that understand the value of cognitive leadership.

Cognitive leaders are, therefore, leaders who can slow down their reactions to situations in ways that allow their brains (mind, will, and emotions) to catch up and then take actions that guide them (and others) to safety. Ergo, people follow them. They consistently create psychological safety that yields the trust of people. Where there is trust, people are more likely to take a risk. Where there is no trust, there is no risk.

Tips to improve your cognitive abilities:

- Take care of yourself mentally and emotionally.
- Challenge your brain. Dendrites are the electrical pathways in our brains. You can form new neural pathways - new ways of thinking.
- Reflect on and evaluate progress.
- Improve your critical thinking skills.
- Read.
- Expose yourself to creative processes and activities.
- Focus on just one thing at a time.

As you gain new experiences, your thinking has the potential to change in subtle but impactful ways. Thinking processes are innovative; they use existing knowledge and generate new insights for current and future applications.

Application:

Practice expanding your thinking in three steps:

Step 1 Evaluate a challenge you face from your perspective. Examine the challenge based on what matters most to you. What is possible from your perspective (your individual perspective or the usual cohort of folks you typically involve in decisions)?

Step 2 Evaluate the same challenge from a broader perspective, as someone or something beyond your perspective. For example, another business unit, community, client, competitor, volunteer, member, dissatisfied customer, another country, gender or demographically different people, etc. Examine the challenge based on what matters most to each of these groups or individuals. What do you believe is possible from their perspective?

Step 3 When you examine the various "others" compared to your perspective, what is different? What is possible now that wasn't possible before you considered the perspectives of others in Step 2?

Three additional points to consider:

• Remain curious. Ask: What's possible?

• Maintain a reputation for having moral character and credibility. Examine your own biases in decision-making and in the engagement of people.

• What are you reading? How are you expanding your circle of influence? How are you challenging yourself and others to remain viable, relevant, and cognitively astute?

Scenario

Carol, Carla, Jerome, and Yao are directors you asked to attend a company-sponsored leadership conference last week. As the Chief of Operations, you asked them to attend the conference and return ready to offer a fresh perspective on key operational challenges. They return with suggestions for changes that would help the company maintain its competitive advantage, but the need to act is now. Carol, who has been with the company longer than anyone, agrees the changes are necessary and would be good, but she points to a number of inefficiencies that would undermine any work that is initiated, and the work would require a significant investment of talent, time, and financial resources. She suggests planning now and holding out until the recession and talent shortages have subsided before taking action, as this is how the company has come through these times in the past. How do you process and resolve this dilemma?

A To remedy the inefficiencies, you brainstorm potential options with the team, test solutions, and use the insights to decide how and when to move forward.

B You agree with Carol and suggest the changes be tabled but ask the team to work behind the scenes on alternative plans. This would prepare you to implement your plans when the economy recovers.

C You do nothing, preferring to wait and see how the economy shifts. This is the safest approach and would prevent you from over-taxing staff who already feel overworked and are burning out.

What is the best response? See the Scenario Answer Key at the end of the Playbook.

PRACTICE PLAN

Complete at least one of these before moving to the next practice:

Set Your Mind: Some of what will be shared in this journal will result in cognitive dissonance; it may contradict what you believe to be true. How will you challenge yourself to push past those internal roadblocks?

Memorize: What will you commit to memory about this practice?

Exercise: Walk through the application and scenario again before moving to the next practice.

REFLECTION

Which insights from this practice most resonated with you?

ACTION PLAN

This is a ☐ 30 ☐ 60 ☐ 90 ☐ 180-day plan.

Start with the Action	The observable measure?	Target Date	Accountability Partner
Example: *Improve my critical thinking skills.*	*Make more logical connections between ideas by asking the questions that lead to useful and effective outcomes.*	*March 30, 20xx*	*C. Jones*

2. BEING **CENTERED** MATTERS.

Case Study

Kara Mann, not the residential and commercial designer, but Kara Mann, the dead-lift strongwoman who, after three attempts, became a national strongman champion, recognized the power of a motivated and centered mind. Just as important as physical preparation is mental preparation and centeredness. She is convinced that the quality of her mental focus at the time of her event has been crucial to her success. "You can't be distracted in the least or paying attention to your opponents." She attributes her success to putting mind over matter.

Much of the psychological and mental health work today is focused on helping one get to a place of being centered, calm, comfortable, and stable that allows them to make logically sound decisions.

In the book **Attached** by Amir Levine and Rachel Heller, the authors refer to people in relationships as being in one of three places: Avoidance, Secure, and Anxious. Similar work done by Susan Brady in the book **Mastering Your Inner Critic** emphasizes the importance of being able to navigate to your compassionate center (self-respect, you are enough) versus being one up (judging others harshly) or one down (judging yourself harshly). Both resources remind us of one thing: we must find a safe place for our recovery, growth, and executive advancement regardless of the environment or situation we face.

Just like in the sports world, there are some executive environments that will build up your brand to add perceived value and increase your credibility, and in others, you may find that being put down is the norm and remaining in the security of a centered mindset is critical. Imagine if Kara had allowed her mind to continually be distracted by her opponents and other external threats? Just as it took Kara three tries to win her competition, it takes time to perfect the skill of being centered.

What time will you give to live a life that knows how to properly handle distractions?

Application:

Curiosity helps you get to your secure center. Practice questions that will help you get there include:

- What am I *really* afraid of?
- What's the worse that will happen?
- So, what if it does?
- Do I lack confidence? If yes, how do I regain it?
- Is it that I know what to do but don't know how to do it? If yes, who can help?
- How can I slow down the process to allow myself to feel secure?
- What am I trying to protect myself from?
- What types of resources will boost my confidence (books, courses, mentors, coaches)?
- What about the culture is influencing my feeling of fear? If I can't influence a culture shift, what can I do?
- What are the things that are within my control? Which things are not?
- Now, what do I need to do with what I know?

Confidence helps you stand firm in your secure center. In what direction is your self-talk taking you - to your secure center or away from it?

You'll know you're not in your secure center when you feel anxious or are avoiding addressing issues. Where do you tend to go in times of stress or pressure?

Scenario

Sonny was offered his dream leadership job. It met his career, salary, and work/life balance needs. He knew it would be a challenge, but he was up for it. After accepting the offer, he received an inside tip that the company was in peril, but outsiders were unaware. The tipster warned him not to take the job, as it would be a terrible career move and possibly hurt his reputation. He decides to take the job and, within 30 days, realizes he has made a grave mistake. Now, six months in, the CEO is increasingly demeaning, reneges on promises made in the job offer, and undermines his every move. Despite his best efforts, he is marginalized and unable to make a difference. He wants to stick it out for a year, fearing it would not look good on his resume to leave before the one-year mark. He has limited savings in the bank and no support system nearby. What would you do?

A You quit and take a temp job if you had to.

B You continue to perform at a high level, practicing centering techniques to help you remain focused. You may also secure trusted advisors such as a coach, mentor, and therapist to help you work through the dilemma. This would help you make an informed rather than an emotional decision about your next step.

C You continue your high level of performance but write a letter and ask to speak with the board chair about the situation. After all, you both hit it off great during the interview process, and he was on the selection committee that hired you. He will be able to provide you with a solution.

What is the best response? See the Scenario Answer Key at the end of the Playbook.

Complete at least one of these before moving to the next practice. Complete all three for deeper impact:

Set Your Mind: Assess your ability to achieve centeredness. What, if anything, needs to happen for you to achieve it?

Memorize: What will you commit to memory about this practice?

Exercise: Walk through the application and scenario again before moving to the next practice. What additional alternatives are viable options for your consideration?

REFLECTION

Which insights from this practice most resonated with you?

....

....

....

....

ACTION PLAN

This is a ☐ 30 ☐ 60 ☐ 90 ☐ 180-day plan.

Start with the Action	The observable measure?	Target Date	Accountability Partner
Example: *Improve my critical thinking skills.*	*Make more logical connections between ideas by asking the questions that lead to useful and effective outcomes.*	*March 30, 20xx*	*C. Jones*

25

3. YOUR **BEHAVIOR** MATTERS.

Case Study

In 1888, a man was shocked and horrified to read his name in the obituary column of the morning paper; the newspapers had erroneously reported his death. When he regained his composure, he was curious to find out what had been said about him. "Dynamite King Dies," the obituary read. And "He was the merchant of death." This man, the inventor of dynamite, asked himself, "Is this how I am going to be remembered, as a purveyor of death?" Disheartened at how he was portrayed, he knew he must make a change. He knew this was not the way he wanted to be remembered. From that day forward, he worked for peace. His name was Alfred Nobel, and he is remembered today for the great Nobel Prize.

Hopefully, you're not being mocked as "the merchant of death," but it does beg the question of the legacy your behavior will bring. Your behavior is the expression of your thoughts and actions in your conduct, attitude, and performance in relation to others. One of the best ways to know how you show up behaviorally is to assess the degree to which you are getting what you set out to get from others. On a scale that ranges from an "angel of light leadership" to the "merchant of death," where does your legacy land?

Executives with a competitive advantage set out to influence their work environment, which results in impacting the lived experiences of others. Those experiences are what dictate their leadership legacy.

Observe those whose conduct, attitude and behaviors are highly esteemed in your organization or your network. What is the difference between their behavior (how they relate to and interact with others) and yours?

If you're unsure, ask for feedback or commission a 360-degree assessment if normal feedback mechanisms are not giving you deep insight.

Next, examine the power dynamics being exerted in the culture:

Coercive power – the leader who resorts to punishment when their demands are not met.

Reward power – the leader who gains compliance through some sort of compensation.

Legitimate power – the leader has the right to have their demands met because of their position.

Referent power – the leader's ability to influence because of their followers' deep respect for them.

Expert power – the leader is seen as an expert and gains respect because of their breadth and depth of knowledge.

Which of these power dynamics are most in use in your culture, which are most effective, and which dynamic are you leveraging most? How is this working for you? What needs to change to boost your effectiveness, credibility, and reputation?

The change framework with regards to executive-level behaviors can be difficult because we often mistakenly believe that what got us here will keep us there. Thus, we say to ourselves, why change?

News Flash: executive-level leadership requires a different set of skills as you move up. The higher you move up in an organization, the less attached you need to be to your individual performance and instead more attached to the performance of the organization.

To change your behavior, you need to change your mind. Here's how:

(A) Identify a behavior change.

Determine the gap between your current state and your desired state as an effective leader and executive. You can do this with a 360-degree assessment. Once you receive the feedback, go back, and ask for clarification in those areas where change is needed without arguing or being defensive. You may need greater context from others, and even though you won't know exactly how someone rated you, select those individuals you trust to give you the most honest feedback. Then, you can use this information to prioritize the changes that are needed.

Practice:

Recall your goal, and each morning remind yourself that you are already a successful leader. Choose adjectives to describe yourself in that future state (effective, influential, respected, ethical, etc.). Attach this statement to your goal. For example, if the feedback suggested a coercive leader and I want to become more of a referent leader, then my morning statement might be "I am already a respected, trusted, and effective leader who actively gains the respect of others." Remember, without a goal, practice will not be meaningful.

(B) Assign meaning to your goal.

By assigning meaning to the change, you instantly engage your neural pathways. What does it mean, how does it feel, what's the personal value? Consider the positive elements of your emotions. If you're considered a micromanager who responds with coercive power when assignments are not achieved by others, while the feedback doesn't feel good, to become more of a referent or expert leader, you can connect the need for change to a positive emotion such as increased respect, trust, and reputation because of the change.

Practice:

Identify a new way of leading. For example, instead of reprimanding people when your demands are not met, you'll practice asking, "What happened, and how will you correct this?" You'll follow this thought every morning by connecting it to the positive outcome such as, "I'll gain respect as a leader," until you know the change has taken place in you.

(C) Reflect, practice, refine and repeat.

The theme of this entire playbook is getting you to exhibit better leadership behaviors. You can only learn a new behavior or skill through practice, and practice creates new neural pathways. Without practice, your brain's glial cells might erase the new message within 24-48 hours or less because it's considered waste.

Practice:

Establish a daily routine of positivity by verbalizing your goals. For example, "Today, I will respond to the interruptions I view as needless with empathy and compassionately convey the best ways for the individual to address the situation or to get on my calendar."

(D) Music and Measurement.

Imagine you must cross a bridge, and this bridge represents your goal. How long it will take depends upon your motivation. What better way to get and stay motivated than by visualizing the outcome? When you do this, studies show, you directly impact your neural pathways. That's right, the retraining of your brain begins at the moment you say go, but remember, to have long-lasting results, you need to cement the changes - and music, which activates the areas of our brain associated with memory, serves to deepen those new practices. Now, look at that goal, imagine what the end looks like, visualize the steps to getting there, load up the music and let it play. If you're like me, you may find that playing music will not only help you achieve goals, but you may get there faster.

Practice:

Each morning, think of your goal. Play your motivational music playlist and visualize yourself achieving your goal. This makes the goal vivid and achievable because it helps your mind, will, and emotions connect positive emotions to the intended outcome. In no time, you'll realize your goals.

(E) Reflection.

I spoke with a mindfulness coach recently, and she put it this way. She said, "Pam, prayer is talking to God, but reflection is listening to God." When you take in an experience, such as a book, podcast, training, or interaction, do you simply walk away and go about the remainder of your day, or do you make meaning (there's that word again) of it by slowing down to clear the clutter and make room for new learning? In this fifth and final step for changing your mind, you must stop casually walking away from essential experiences and instead pause and listen to what is happening within you. If you were a visitor in someone's house, how would you feel if no one made room for you or engaged you in conversation? That's what this final step is about. You're welcoming a guest who probably needs to stay awhile. Will you ignore them or engage them long enough to make them feel at home?

Practice:

Following each day, each training experience, or each chapter you read in a book or article in a magazine, your brain needs time to consider it. Spend 10-15 minutes sitting with it, reflecting upon the information you've read, and stabilizing your mind. This is one of the most effective mental training methods you can engage in for the achievement of your goals. So, what will you do after reading this practice?

Not only have I provided you with the tools, but I've given you examples of how to use them. It's your move. We all have areas of our brand that need a little rewiring. What's holding you back?

Application:

- Identify a goal and start the rewiring process as described above. You will have struggles. Get comfortable with discomfort and let the retraining begin.
- Inclusive leaders challenge their own way of thinking, their own biases, and build culturally diverse teams. Self-awareness, coaching, and mentoring can help.
- In what ways are you too attached to your own performance instead of the performance of the organization? To what extent are you willing to move talent and shift resources to meet the need of the organization, even if it means a debit to your own department or division?
- What's getting in the way of thinking in this manner? This could be the clue to a needed shift in your behavior.

4. ACCOUNTABILITY
MATTERS.

Case Study

One organization had a public brand that did not match its private brand. The CEO had grown up in the organization and was exhibiting outdated and, at times, unethical leadership behaviors. The turnover at all levels was alarming, and even under the threat of media coverage, the board did nothing. A leader of the organization called and asked, "Pam, what do you do when the board doesn't hold the CEO accountable for their behavior?"

My reply: RUN

Boards are accountable to financial institutions, funders, investors, customers, members, bodies of accreditation, regulators, courts, and to themselves as representatives of the organization. Resolving situations like these can take a fair amount of time - if the organization and leadership are not crushed under the weight of the situation first. When faced with a situation in which the problem is bad board governance, you'll have to make a decision about how you want your brand and your reputation to be known. If you can't put the fire out, the longer you stay near it, the more you'll smell like smoke.

Regardless, whether you're in a board seat, an executive seat, or another leadership seat, leading people is challenging. Therefore, expectations must be established if you expect them to hold themselves accountable. This means they are willing to accept the accolades for a job well done and to accept the consequences when the job is done poorly.

Pause for a moment: when was the last time you addressed the potential consequences of a failed effort?

Seeking New Opportunities

When you seek new opportunities, make sure to review the job and clarify expectations, be sure to include YOUR standard for excellence, invite them to share their idea of excellence, and then agree on the expected outcome. A discussion of your standards for excellence and the potential consequences creates shared meaning and improves the likelihood of achieving strategic intent.

There are at least six major non-negotiable expectations executives should have and communicate to their direct reports:

Commitment
Cooperation
Consideration
Communication
Contribution
Consequences

To do this, use our APSEA™ method for communicating these and other expectations.

A – Articulate each item (briefly).

P = Pause and listen for their contribution to each of the expectations.

S = Show support for their ability to meet expectations and achieve goals.

E = Explore obstacles and options (this is a must, or you'll find yourself repeatedly revisiting this list).

A = Action and accountability (ask them to tell you the signs that they are disengaged and how to help them get refocused. Also, ask how they will hold themselves accountable).

Ask for a written summary paragraph of what they believe are the expectations for the assignment.

Key Accountability Practices

Hold people accountable for both actions and results.
For example, if someone says they are going to make calls, then those calls are "actions." If they make calls and close sales, then those are results. You're tracking for actions and results.

If they fail, there MUST be consequences.
If you don't hold people accountable for keeping performance standards, then you'll find you're not getting the results you need. Plus, you lose leadership credibility.

Expectations are NOT Negotiable.
When your standards slip, then so will their performance.

Be Consistent
Accountability requires consistency - don't enforce it at one time but then not another.

Application:

Here's a simple hack coaches use to help clients establish self-accountability that you can use too. At the conclusion of an accountability session with direct reports, close the discussion by asking,

"So, when we meet again in xyz days or weeks, you assure me that you will have made the stated improvements, achievements, or outcomes, correct?"

Thank them and reaffirm your trust that they will do what they have agreed to.

Next, close the meeting a little early and ask them to send you an email briefly describing the challenge or assignment, their plan of action, and how they will hold themselves accountable for meeting the deadline.

Reiterate that this email needs to be brief and to the point. Teach people how to make the best use of your time by directing them how NOT to write manifestos for every assignment given.

Scenario

ABC Company's top competitor, XYZ LLC, just announced the release of its new product, having innovative features that threaten to take a significant market share and customers away from ABC. The announcement sent shock waves through ABC, and as CEO, Aran feels compelled to make an immediate response. With a pending Board meeting next week, he will need to answer pressing questions about how ABC will respond to this surprising news, including how to protect revenue while still serving customers.

ABC has a product under development that is six months away from release, but it has yet to be tested to ensure it lives up to ABC's reputation as a company with quality products for its loyal customers. How should Aran respond to this news? Which option demonstrates the most significant accountability to the organization?

A Unilaterally announce to the Board of Directors and the press that ABC will release their product within six weeks, and it will be equal to or better than XYZ's product.

B Consult with the product development team about XYZ's news and define new expectations for product delivery, sharing the potential revenue and market share consequences for sticking to the original 6-month timeline.

C Demand that the product development team work overtime and skip routine quality control testing so they can deliver the product in four weeks.

What is the best response? See the Scenario Answer Key at the end of the Playbook.

PRACTICE PLAN

Complete at least one of these before moving to the next practice. Complete all three for deeper impact:

Set Your Mind: Of the behaviors above, which one(s) are you wrestling with? What will you set your mind to change?

Memorize: What will you commit to memory about this practice?

Exercise: Walk through the APSEA™ method with someone before moving to the next practice.

REFLECTION

Which insights from this practice most resonated with you?

....

....

....

....

ACTION PLAN

This is a ☐ 30 ☐ 60 ☐ 90 ☐ 180-day plan.

Start with the Action	The observable measure?	Target Date	Accountability Partner
Example: *Improve my critical thinking skills.*	*Make more logical connections between ideas by asking the questions that lead to useful and effective outcomes.*	*March 30, 20xx*	*C. Jones*

5. COACHING MATTERS.

--- Case Study ---

"I needed someone to guide me in the right direction to becoming a successful leader. Pam was every bit of what I needed and more. She made me realize I was already a successful leader; I just needed to realize it and believe it! She dug deep and forced me to think outside the box, causing me to face myself and uncover the "why" do you think you're not a leader, to get to the "how" will you show up as a leader." - Happy Client

How do you know you need growth? Who told you? Why do you believe it? What do you want to do about it? These are all questions you could be asked by a coach, someone who can help you work on yourself. Coaching and mentoring are musts for those in or who are advancing to executive leadership. Mentors are useful in providing you with experiential insights, while coaches teach you how to think your way through situational roadblocks. Sponsors ensure you advocate for those with talent, credibility, and capability who struggle for visibility and recognition of their talent - typically women and people of color. Let's explore all three.

MENTORS

Look for a mentor when you want to speak with someone who has specific skills and expertise. EVERY executive needs a mentor:

- Who has been there and done that?

- Who has the kind of experience that will act as a blueprint for your own success?

- Who can share with you their wisdom and knowledge in a specific topic area?

- Who can you learn from because they have almost all of the information you need to move forward?

In your mentor relationship, it is all about the mentor. Your mentor knows you value their experience and expertise, and they plan to spend time with you to tell you about their experiences – the focus of the conversation is on them. Your mentor is in the driver's seat of the interaction.

Self-check: Who is your mentor, and whom are you mentoring?

COACHES

Coaching is most effective when you need someone to help you focus on your individual development:

- You're blazing new trails or going somewhere you've not gone before.

- You're stuck and unsure of your next move.

- You need someone who can help you make sense of all the chaos you're experiencing personally and professionally.

- You need help dealing with self-sabotaging behaviors that disrupt your dreams and want a coach to help you recognize and move beyond those barriers.

- You expect the outcome to be much more or better than what you might have achieved on your own.

- You don't need a subject matter expert to tell you what to do, but you need someone experienced in helping people get motivated and hold themselves accountable for their goals.

In a coaching relationship, it is all about you. Your coach knows how to successfully explore possibilities and reveal your potential with confidence enough to put you in the driver's seat of the conversation without advice and judgment. Your coach's sole responsibility will be to help you move beyond your current perceived limits through powerful questioning, insights, creating awareness, and designing actions.

Self-check: When was the last time you worked with a coach?

Sponsorship at the executive level is critical and valuable because it reveals talented and high-potential employees that might be otherwise focused on the consistent development of their technical skills. Sponsorship is a practice that benefits both the talent and the organization.

Sponsorship works like this: remember the movie, *Jerry Maguire*? Well, if you're already an executive, then you're the sport's agent. You're not the coach, not the family member, not the best friend. You're examining all the draft picks and trying to determine who is number one and how you can entice them to your organization. You're the one looking for the next best opportunity for the employee you're sponsoring. To do that, you need to get clear on what is needed organizationally and what the talent (the next-level employee) has to offer. This way, when an opportunity presents itself, you are in the best position to advocate for that next-level leader.

If you are not in an executive seat, then you want to position yourself as a senior leader's number one draft pick. Whom do you know, and who needs to know you? In what ways are you interfering in your own lack of visibility? Go back to the book, ***Think Like a Brand*** and read Step Five: Grow Strategic Brand Visibility to learn more.

Self-check: Whom are you sponsoring?

Application:

When you negotiate for your next opportunity, make sure you request the company invest in a coach for you that you select for your first six months to 1-year in that role.

(A) In selecting a coach, here are some important interview questions:

1. What is your coaching specialty? What areas do you most often work with?

Coaches typically specialize or consistently work in certain areas. Look for those areas that you relate to. Finding a coach that specializes in something that directly relates to you and your situation is preferable, but don't allow it to be the only deciding factor. A well-rounded background can be helpful.

2. What is your coaching approach or philosophy?

Listen for the coach's emphasis on capacity building, not problem-solving. The coach's overall philosophy should revolve around building your capacity to achieve your goals and objectives.

3. What are some of your coaching success stories?

Ask for some specific examples of individuals who have done well. You are looking to see if your ideas of success match. Can you picture yourself as the next success story with this coach?

When working with a coach, to make the best use of your time, think about the one thing you want to tackle, one topic to cover, or an outcome to achieve by the end of your coaching session. Usually, this helps you feel a sense of accomplishment with each session.

(B) **If you have a coach and are looking for a deeper experience, take a moment and ask your coach: How can I get more out of our sessions?**

Scenario

After growing with a large global consumer products firm, Bella's long-time sponsor reached out to her with a new opportunity to move to the US from her home in Latin America. Bella's experience would add not only cultural diversity at headquarters, but they would lean on her expertise with the Latin American market. She was excited at both the personal and professional opportunities in addition to connecting with her peers in the US.

Upon arrival, Bella was assigned a coach by the HR team. After the first two meetings, it was apparent that Bella did not connect well with her coach, who told her to "just give it time." She discovered that her coach was someone who had never coached employees outside of the US. Bella felt that she needed more from her coach but didn't want to cancel her next meeting. What should she do at her next coaching appointment?

A Contact HR and demand a new coach who better understands Bella's situation and cancel the appointment if she does not get a new coach.

B Keep the appointment, but ask the current coach about their coaching philosophy, success with previous employees in Bella's situation, and expectations for the future.

C Call her sponsor and ask what she should do.

What is the best response? See the Scenario Answer Key at the end of the Playbook.

Complete at least one of these before moving to the next practice. Complete all three for deeper impact:

Set Your Mind: If you don't have a coach, what are your plans for securing one? What benefits are you gaining from working with a coach? Whom are you mentoring? At this level, it is time to give back. Even if you're at the top of your game, a CEO perhaps, you need to keep a coach handy and a mentor nearby.

Memorize: What will you commit to memory about this practice?

Exercise: Select and apply either Application A or Application B before moving to the next practice.

REFLECTION

Which insights from this practice most resonated with you?

....

....

....

....

ACTION PLAN

This is a ☐ 30 ☐ 60 ☐ 90 ☐ 180-day plan.

Start with the Action	The observable measure?	Target Date	Accountability Partner
Example: *Improve my critical thinking skills.*	*Make more logical connections between ideas by asking the questions that lead to useful and effective outcomes.*	*March 30, 20xx*	*C. Jones*

PHASE 2:
LEADING OTHERS

1. LEADERSHIP **STYLES** MATTER.

Case Study

After 18 months on the job, I was promoted to a C-suite position. It was a highly coveted and highly competitive internal position. We all knew someone internally would get it, but as it was told to me by a then peer, "You'll never get that job; it's owed to someone else who's been here longer." Well, one of those "someones" was a peer who would prove to be very challenging at first. She would undermine me in front of members of our team and, of course, behind the scenes. One day, I said to myself, "Maybe I should just give her the darn job." That's when the lightbulbs went off. I knew she'd continue to undermine my ability to lead the team if I didn't give her what she wanted. So, I gave her a significant chunk of the business - a very important assignment with the full-on access, visibility, and accountability she and others so desperately wanted for her. After six months, she decided she didn't want it and was glad I was the person who got the job.

To give her that authority, I had to:

1. Adopt other leadership styles. I had first to lead myself and work through my emotional baggage.

2. Remember that I was leading others, and they were watching - all of them - those in my corner and those who were not.

3. Realize that this was about the organization, and we would not get anything done with dissension among the ranks. Mastery of all three was required.

Self-awareness

Awareness is the beginning of change and overseeing yourself and your behaviors. When leaders step into executive roles, they often rely on past behaviors to achieve new outcomes. However, while change is inevitable, growth - increased capacity- is optional. Growth is intentional, not accidental. You must decide to grow and accept its lessons. Otherwise, you remain stuck constantly feeling defeated, but you don't have to. Growth doesn't mean agreement with the required changes. It just means you are willing to adjust your own conduct, attitude, and behavior to accommodate the changes.

Start by recognizing what your emotions want you to do or not to do. Emotion is the impulse to do something. When a change is presented, your emotions want you to agree with and adjust to the change, fight the change, or sit in limbo, unclear about the change. Learn how to identify the voice in your head. It can drive out your ability to think rationally. If you lack an awareness of your strengths, weaknesses, opportunities, and threats (for your brand), then your effectiveness will diminish, and your ability to recognize and adjust the dial on your emotions to fit the situation will be rendered ineffective.

Next, conduct a proper SWOT (strength, weakness, opportunity, threat) analysis to begin the process of strengthening your ability to change and adapt to business needs. Consider a SWOT analysis as your personal threat assessment to gain clarity on the things you do well and the things you're doing that will undermine the things you do well. However, be aware that most people believe a SWOT analysis stands alone as both an internal and external environmental scan and a strategic framework, and it does not. In part, it can be used as a strategic framework, but not without some customization. Therefore, below, I've outlined the questions you can answer to conduct your personal SWOT, Step 1. Step 2 is then leveraging the TOWS (threat, opportunity, weakness, strength) method to extend value to the SWOT and make it more actionable.

Step 1 SWOT Evaluation Method

STRENGTHS

- What is it that you do exceptionally well?
- What are the types of challenges that others ask you to resolve most?
- What do people say they love and admire most about working with/being around you?

WEAKNESSES

- What aspects of your personality may be holding you back?
- What negative habits do you have?
- What are the gaps in your talent, skills, and abilities?

OPPORTUNITIES

- Is there a need in your department, the organization, or the market that is going unfulfilled?
- What can you do that is unique, better, or different today that isn't being done?
- What new technology, insight, or resource can help you achieve your goals?

THREATS

- Where do you make the most mistakes?
- How are you managing your health? To what extent will your health management practices enable or prevent you from achieving your goals?
- To what extent are you aware of current or impending changes in your field (or the organization) that could threaten your success?

Step 2 TOWS Threat Assessment and Action Plan

Failing to evaluate the threats you've assessed in your SWOT is where most leaders fall short. Move to the head of the class by conducting a TOWS or similar assessment to gain the full value of your SWOT.

Address each statement in the box below:

STRENGTHS: OPPORTUNITIES	WEAKNESSES: OPPORTUNITIES
Match one strength to one opportunity and write how you will use that strength to realize that opportunity.	Match one opportunity to one weakness and write how you will use the opportunity to overcome or improve upon that weakness.

STRENGTHS: THREATS	WEAKNESSES: THREATS
Match one threat to one strength and write how you will use that strength to reduce, avoid, or eliminate the threat.	What strategies can you employ to eliminate or avoid threats and minimize or overcome weaknesses?

Discipline at Critical Moments

Leaders repeatedly face tough decisions where the answer isn't readily apparent. These decisions pull on your conceptual expertise more than any capability, and emotional intelligence helps discipline your conduct, attitude, and behavior during those demanding times.

Critical moments don't always give us advanced notice. When they emerge, you must be prepared to act. What makes the moment critical is often not the decision itself but the emotion that comes with having to decide when how you feel does not align with what you need to do. Every leader will be faced with having to do things that are not comfortable. Get in the habit of embracing productive discomfort.

How prepared are you to make decisions at critical moments?

- To what extent have you/can you interrupt negative thoughts? When has this occurred? What was the outcome?

- When was the last time you redirected your focus to being present and in the moment? What was happening? What was the value?

- What do you say to yourself when you need to replace negative self-talk with positive self-talk?

LEADING OTHERS

Being attached to one style of leading is what ruins some of the most capable individuals. They believe, mistakenly, that what got them to the next level will keep them there. Now that we know we must change our leadership style as our position changes, it is time to be practicing various ways of leading.

Which is your go-to leadership style?

1. Autocratic (authoritarian) - make all the decisions / follow me
2. Pacesetting - drive fast results
3. Democratic - everyone has a voice
4. Coaching - empowers others
5. Laissez-Faire - trusts others to do their jobs
6. Visionary - sees clearly how the future should look
7. Servant - people first
8. Transformational -big picture, help people see what's possible
9. Bureaucratic - rule followers, very procedural
10. Transactional - day-to-day and hierarchical leaders

Each of these styles is useful for the right situation. Knowing how to apply different skills to each situation is important for your sustainable success.

LEADING THE ORGANIZATION

Competitive Advantage is the extent to which you can efficiently and effectively produce goods or services that result in your ability to outperform your competitors. The foundation of any competitive advantage includes superior quality, efficiency, responsiveness to clients or customers, innovation, talent, and the organization's culture.

To lead an organization towards the achievement of or maintaining a competitive advantage, you'll have to ensure your systems of accountability for planning, organizing, leading, and controlling are sound. You cannot skip this step and believe you'll maintain a competitive advantage.

PLANNING

involves the selection and establishment of goals, strategies, and the allocation of resources.

ORGANIZING

involves the design of structures, processes, and systems to facilitate the interconnection of the talent for optimal individual, team, and organizational performance.

LEADING

requires the creation and communication of a compelling vision that promotes and motivates a high level of performance.

CONTROLLING

is an evaluation of the organization's performance and the actions needed to correct, improve, or maintain standards of performance.

FINAL CHECK - Make sure employees know:

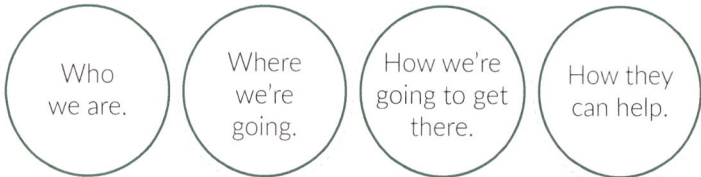

Who we are.

Where we're going.

How we're going to get there.

How they can help.

Application:

What is your leadership style now? If you were in my shoes, as described in the case study above, how would you have handled that situation? Perhaps there is a different or similar situation you face.

What do your SWOT and your TOWS (from the Leading Self section) tell you are your potential blind spots, things that could rob you of your credibility and success as an effective executive?

What combinations of styles does the culture demand of you? Which will be most challenging? How will you address this?

In his previous role as CEO of a startup software company, Gerald was known as a maverick. He had a decisive no-holds-barred approach that grew revenue by 400% in less than two years. He was used to everyone following his orders, knowing that the grueling demands of a startup required his keenly focused, goal-oriented approach.

Gerald was hired as a turnaround CEO for a mature software company and was certain that his entrepreneurial and autocratic style would benefit his new employer. Instead, he was met with resistance from an executive team who valued inclusion and wanted to move forward with a more strategic, well-planned approach that people understood before they started. Gerald was initially optimistic that his maverick tendencies would shake up the organization, but he found these new expectations frustrating, slowing down his plans. Should Gerald:

A Insist that his approach is best for the company, require they follow his direction and trust that he knows what is best based on his past performance.

B Evaluate how his autocratic, maverick style has both strengths and weaknesses that may be holding him back.

C Let the executive team do what they think is best and report back to Gerald with their results.

What is the best response? See the Scenario Answer Key at the end of the Playbook.

PRACTICE PLAN

Complete at least one of these before moving to the next practice. Complete all three for deeper impact:

Set Your Mind: Which of the three "leading" areas are in most need of your attention? Why? What will you commit to?

Memorize: What will you commit to memory about this practice?

Exercise: Walk through the application and scenario again before moving to the next practice.

REFLECTION

Which insights from this practice most resonated with you?

....

....

....

....

ACTION PLAN

This is a ☐ 30 ☐ 60 ☐ 90 ☐ 180-day plan.

Start with the Action	The observable measure?	Target Date	Accountability Partner
Example: Improve my critical thinking skills.	*Make more logical connections between ideas by asking the questions that lead to useful and effective outcomes.*	*March 30, 20xx*	*C. Jones*

2. YOUR **COMMUNICATION** MATTERS.

He kept walking and never spoke another word about her behavior. From that day forward, I started watching and listening more closely in board meetings. I realized that we are always communicating. Even when we don't say a word. No arguing. Allowing stupidity to have the last words. Refusing to lose your temper and maintaining emotional control are powerful communication methods that they mastered. Had they engaged her foolishness on the day my ego crash-landed, we might never have gotten out of there, and hurtful unprofessional things might have been said. In truth, that experience taught me three valuable lessons:

1	**2**	**3**
We are ALWAYS communicating.	There's always someone watching you.	Sometimes it's a good thing to let others have the last word.

One definition of communication is the skillful and deliberate exchange of information to the degree that the intended message is actually received. Skillful and deliberate. Skillful people know how to use body language, facial expressions, tone, pitch, and silence to communicate. In fact, they seek to know in advance what they're up against, and so they plan how they are going to interact and respond. When they don't know, to retain their credibility, they intentionally guide conversations and interactions to an expected end.

Is your method of communication hurting your credibility?

1. Are you unwilling to admit mistakes?

2. Do you share too much information?

3. Do you lack self-awareness and deliberation when communicating?

4. Do poor diction or grammatically incorrect writing plague your brand?

5. Do you withhold important information during critical times?

6. Are you communicating micro-aggressively?

7. Are you known to miss the mark and deliver the wrong messages?

8. Does your fear of delivering bad news hurt your credibility?

9. Are you communicating on the fly rather than with the support of a communication plan?

10. Do receivers of your communication have trouble accepting and understanding the message?

Key Questions:

Improving how you relate to and communicate with others requires a regimen of 4 key questions:

a. Who is my audience?
b. What value am I adding to the relationship?
c. What is the experience I want others to have because of working with me?
d. How can I best connect to make an impact?

Remember, the ability to communicate is not one-sided. However, the pressure to establish and hold ourselves and others accountable for effective communication is vital and often rests on your shoulders. Set the expectations that your "others" need to bring their insights and ideas to contribute to the conversation in meaningful ways. Otherwise, you fall into a rut in your approach to leading, missing the opportunity to create new neural pathways for yourself and others.

Self-check:

Unsure how you show up as a communicator? Here's a self-check to help you evaluate yourself:

1. Before you attend a meeting, formal or informal, do you give considerable thought to what you're going to say? How you're going to engage?
2. To what extent do you anticipate and deliberate on potential negative interactions?
3. Do you anticipate and prepare for responses?
4. Do you primarily engage in one-way or two-way conversations?
5. Do you know the most effective form of communication for each of your key stakeholders?
6. Are your responses typically fact or opinion-based?
7. Are your body language and positioning conveying your level of interest and engagement? Front of the room vs. back, lean in or sit back?
8. Is your communication clear and concise?

9. Do you consider the feelings and emotions of the person with whom you are communicating?

10. Do you encourage feedback on your suggestions and ideas?

11. Do you adjust your communication style according to the person with whom you are speaking?

12. Are you intentional about creating a positive impression? Do you just walk in, or are you "showing up"?

13. Do you effectively use humor and candor to keep the conversation open?

14. Are you able to tailor your communication to the type of meeting you're in?

How would you rate your effectiveness as a communicator? Place a circle around those items you know you'll need to work on and engage the services of a coach to help.

Application:

Here's a sample outline for a communication strategy that can help you achieve executive advantage:

A. What is the purpose of the communication?

Is the purpose intellectual in nature (you're sharing knowledge and information), is it inspirational (you want to motivate or inspire staff), or both?

B. What is the intent and desired impact of the communication?

Is the communication intended for business or interpersonal use, and are we saying what's important when it matters most?

C. Do we want to encourage feedback?

Typically, if the communication is unilateral, no feedback is needed or expected. For bilateral communication, you want to encourage the exchange of information and feedback from others.

Regardless, remain open to questions, comments, and concerns. Employees prefer dialogue over the feeling of being lectured or on the other side of a lengthy monologue. Adults want engagement and the feeling of having a voice, even if they choose not to use it.

D. How official is the message? Should the message be delivered formally or informally?

E. Which communication channels will we use?

(Face to face) (Video/ televised) (Mobile) (Written) (Electronic)

F. Which delivery format will we use?

For example - briefings, full written reports or abstracts, executive summaries, brochures, press releases, talking points, verbal messaging, press conferences, articles or other publications, town halls, etc.

G. Who will communicate which messages and when?

Often there is a cascading communication process, and other times there are simultaneous message strategies. Critical messages with calls to action are often best communicated by the group leader closest to those who must take the action. Get clear on who will communicate which message, how and what will be the timing for doing so:

(Board Chair) (CEO) (Senior Leaders) (Spokes-person) (People Managers)

H. Do we include a call to action (CTA)?

Provide closure for employees by telling them what to do or expect and to whom they should direct their questions or comments.

I. Is the language short and simple?

Avoid ambiguous language and business or industry jargon when not needed. Your messaging should be kept brief and to the point.

J. Measure: Is your strategy working?

• Which methods work best?

• Are employees feeling more/less engaged and informed?

• Track opens and responses.

• Measure CTA's: Is action being taken?

Jules was known for his candor as VP of Finance. He knew numbers inside and out and forwarded his timely and detailed P&L statements before every board meeting. Ready to defend his position against company expansion, he never understood why Board Members looked at him with glazed eyes when he spoke. They were not engaged, but Jules knew the information he presented was essential to the company's future. If he didn't start communicating in a way that the CEO and Board Members clearly understood, Jules feared that the company would make ill-advised decisions threatening its future viability. To correct this problem, Jules should:

A Communicate the top five most important findings of his report while saving half of his presentation time to answer questions from Board Members and senior leadership.

B Speak more loudly, adding more intense body language to accentuate important financial points while maintaining eye contact with the Board President during his 40-page detailed presentation.

C Practice his presentation before his peers from other company divisions to get their advice on presenting his findings better. If they present advice Jules doesn't like, he can disregard it.

What is the best response? See the Scenario Answer Key at the end of the Playbook.

Complete at least one of these before moving to the next practice. Complete all three for deeper impact:

Set Your Mind: Communication can be challenging even for the best communicators. Think seriously about your communication efforts. What needs your intense focus and attention?

Memorize: What will you commit to memory about this practice?

Exercise: Walk through the application above. Decide where the gaps exist in your communication and practice something new before moving to the next practice.

REFLECTION

Which insights from this practice most resonated with you?

....

....

....

....

ACTION PLAN

This is a ☐ 30 ☐ 60 ☐ 90 ☐ 180-day plan.

Start with the Action	The observable measure?	Target Date	Accountability Partner
Example: *Improve my critical thinking skills.*	*Make more logical connections between ideas by asking the questions that lead to useful and effective outcomes.*	*March 30, 20xx*	*C. Jones*

3. **CONFLICT** LEADERSHIP MATTERS.

--- **Case Study** ---

Years ago, when my husband and I were searching for a home, we engaged in so much conflict that the poor realtor just thought we weren't ready until I told her, "Oh, don't worry about us. You'll know we've found the house when there's more agreement than disagreement." Sure enough, we eventually walked into our "agreement" house, and she said, "Well, I'm guessing this is the house?" and she was right because there was way more agreement than disagreement.

It's safe to say that no one enjoys conflict, and I would be remiss not to address it in this playbook. Conflict is an integral part of creative discourse and even normal interaction. It emerges, and almost without thinking, we react.

Conflict is an opportunity that screams **STOP, THINK**, and then asks, **WHAT'S THE OPPORTUNITY HERE?**

Think about this as it relates to leading people. Conflict is healthy when it leads you to a place of agreement, but it can take nerves of steel and some simple conflict management skills to get there.

Embrace conflict as an opportunity for coaching and learning. The only bad conflict is conflict that goes unresolved. By embracing conflict and adopting a coaching culture, you will boost productivity and reduce the negative effects of conflict in the organization.

Here are some tips to help you address these experiences:

Explore what's going on.

Allow all parties to talk through what they are thinking or feeling. Allow them to discuss their perspectives. This is where conflict coaching is extremely helpful and can eliminate additional conflicts escalating. When all involved parties are allowed to share their views, opinions, and ideas in a safe space, the potential for new and improved processes to emerge is high.

Expand the landscape.

A problem or conflict is never just two-sided; there is always another way out. Expand the possible alternatives by encouraging the parties in conflict to work together to identify other potential solutions. Establishing common ground helps diminish the conflict, takes their focus away from their own worldview, and expands their thinking in creative ways.

Express new learnings.

Accountability is critical in sustaining conflict resolution. Use these types of coaching questions to immediately cement the learning and sustained resolution of issues: What have you learned about yourself? What have you learned about others? How will you hold yourself accountable for long-term change? What steps will you take in the future to quickly resolve new conflicts?

Don't allow a situation to get to a boiling point before attempting to diffuse it, but if it does: **Explore, Expand and Express.**

Application:

If you have to address conflict, here are some questions to help you work through the situation:

- What is the conflict (from all perspectives)?
- What is the conflict costing the organization?
- What behaviors are hurting the situation?
- What behaviors are needed to overcome and successfully arrest the conflict?
- What possibilities are available for moving forward?
- Which is the best option to select?
- What could prevent you from reaching your intended outcome/ goal?

- What personal changes do you think you would have to make to achieve your goal?
- What will be the observable signs of success – short-term and long-term?
- What have we learned from this experience?
- How can we avoid a repeat of this scenario?

As you can see, while these are just a few core questions to work through conflict, they are effective on their own. From this point, have the individual that you are working through the conflict conversation with write up how they will work through the conflict and hold themselves accountable for improved behaviors.

Following a pattern of conflict management like this will ensure that, ultimately, individuals can work through conflict on their own.

Scenario

From their first days as new employees over ten years ago, Victoria and Oliver never got along. Everyone could see that they were more alike than not, each having strong opinions while insisting their ideas were better than their peer. Their aggressive drive for results made them experts in their respective departments, but now that they held similar positions, both Regional General Manager of the East Coast and West Coast, they suddenly found that they no longer were expected to compete but to cooperate to drive sales for the entire organization.

As the business environment took a turn for the worse, the CEO, their immediate superior, asked Victoria and Oliver to develop a plan that offered best sales practices to grow revenue. How should Victoria and Oliver develop a plan that the entire company depends on to serve over 1,000 employees and 10,000 customers?

A   Spend weeks negotiating on whose turf they should meet, under what terms, and for how long.

B   Challenge each person to make a list of the top 10 best practices that work in each of their regions, including measured results, choose the best ideas, and then present a plan to the CEO.

C   Have Victoria and Oliver each insist on having a private conversation with the CEO to explain why their approach is better than their peer.

What is the best response? See the Scenario Answer Key at the end of the Playbook.

PRACTICE PLAN

Complete at least one of these before moving to the next practice. Complete all three for deeper impact:

Set Your Mind: Of the three E's (explore, expand, and express) for addressing conflict, where do you struggle most? What will you do?

Memorize: What will you commit to memory about this practice?

Exercise: Walk through the application and scenario again before moving to the next practice. In fact, conflict is inevitable, so wait for it to emerge and practice one new way to manage the conflict before moving to the next practice.

REFLECTION

Which insights from this practice most resonated with you?

....

....

....

....

ACTION PLAN

This is a ☐ 30 ☐ 60 ☐ 90 ☐ 180-day plan.

Start with the Action	The observable measure?	Target Date	Accountability Partner
Example: Improve my critical thinking skills.	*Make more logical connections between ideas by asking the questions that lead to useful and effective outcomes.*	*March 30, 20xx*	*C. Jones*

4. **COLLABORATION** MATTERS.

Case Study

Edison is most famous for his development of the first electric light bulb. Yet, what some fail to recall about his story is that some of his inventions were improvements on other inventions, like the telephone. In fact, while he holds more patents than any other person in U.S. history, he invented and built many of his inventions with other people. It's Edison's invention factory that makes him widely held as the pioneer of teamwork.

Today, collaboration is both widely elusive and widely sought after. Why? Because when it works, it works! Collaboration occurs when individuals work together to achieve a defined common business purpose. When individuals can't work together to achieve organizational goals, silos and passive-aggressive behaviors move into place and become the "norm" for how the work does not get accomplished.

You'll know your collaboration efforts are successful if they result in:

- Increased diversity of thought
- Strategic drift avoidance
- Identification of potential and real threats
- Innovation and creativity
- Improved efficiencies and effectiveness

Knowing **WHEN** to collaborate is equally important, for example:

| Generate new ideas and spark innovation | Addressing and resolving risk and complexities | Planning and strategizing |

Collaborations often lead to a need for change. However, most organizations fail miserably when it comes to change management, and the failed change effort then results in unnecessary finger-pointing. To remedy this, choose a change management strategy you can adopt internally and apply it to your change efforts. There are several to consider:

- ADKAR Change Management Model
- Bridges' Transition Model
- Kotter's 8-Step Theory
- Kübler-Ross Change Curve
- Lewin's Change Management Model
- Maurer 3 Levels of Resistance and Change Model
- McKinsey 7-S Model

There are five critical elements that will pave the way for successful collaboration efforts:

Awareness. Successful collaborators know that being aware of and adjusting their communication style as needed not only equips them with confidence and credibility but also helps them achieve a higher level of intelligence.

Think: How would you rate yourself when it comes to being self-aware? What adjustments will you need to practice to ensure everyone has a chance to participate in the collaboration effort?

Agreement and shared understanding are amongst the easiest elements needed to get people to work together but are often the most overlooked.

Think: How can I help everyone come to an agreement about what needs to happen next? How can I refrain from getting hung up on my own opinions, wants, and desires in favor of what is best for the organization?

Acknowledge (and celebrate) the contributions of others.

Think: It's not about me; it's about us. What are we doing, and how can I celebrate the contributions of individuals who helped us achieve our goals?

Allow space for and encourage healthy discourse. Every successful outcome must pass through conflict to achieve success, but not all conflict is bad. Learn easy communication methods to leverage differences in opinions and stay on course.

Think: How can I disagree without being disagreeable? Which conflict reconciliation practices shared here in this journal, or others you've used, can you adopt to resolve and learn from any conflict that will emerge?

Accountability used to be elusive, but only because leaders took too much responsibility for establishing accountability. You don't hold others accountable until they first agree to hold themselves accountable.

Think: How can I make it a habit of holding myself accountable and modeling that behavior for others when collaborating?

Finally, to create clear lines of responsibility in the collaboration effort, consider a decision matrix such as the RACI model:

R	A	C	I
Who is Responsible for ongoing tasks and assignments?	Who holds ultimate Accounta-bility for the outcome?	Who will need to be Consulted along the way?	Who needs to be kept Informed about our progress?

Models such as these create role clarity throughout the collaboration effort.

Application:

What are the challenges you and others in your organization face when it comes to collaboration? Discuss them at your next meeting.

Who in the organization exhibits good collaboration skills? How can you leverage them?

Scenario

Dimitri feels the pressure of leading a mature organization with products that serve an eroding membership base. At the last Board Meeting, the Directors discussed the need for the organization to become more innovative, offer leading-edge options, and attract new, younger members. As CEO, Dimitri knows his departments need to be more collaborative, but his Vice Presidents get stuck in defending their silos and don't have incentives to work together. To get the ball rolling, Dimitri should:

A Sponsor a weekend retreat with all his Vice Presidents to brainstorm ideas for new products and services, hiring an outside professional facilitator to guide the discussions. At the end of the meeting, they would create a list of people responsible for putting these new ideas into action.

B Hire a consultant to tell Dimitri what new products and services they should produce and give the list to his Vice Presidents to make it happen.

C Have a company-wide contest to offer new product and service ideas.

What is the best response? See the Scenario Answer Key at the end of the Playbook.

Complete at least one of these before moving to the next practice. Complete all three for deeper impact:

Set Your Mind: What plans, strategies, and/or potential risks could benefit from improved collaboration? What action will you take?

Memorize: What will you commit to memory about this practice?

Exercise: Walk through the application and scenario again before moving to the next practice.

REFLECTION

Which insights from this practice most resonated with you?

....

....

....

....

ACTION PLAN

This is a ☐ 30 ☐ 60 ☐ 90 ☐ 180-day plan.

Start with the Action	The observable measure?	Target Date	Accountability Partner
Example: Improve my critical thinking skills.	Make more logical connections between ideas by asking the questions that lead to useful and effective outcomes.	March 30, 20xx	C. Jones

5. **DELEGATION** MATTERS.

Case Study

I had an executive assistant who once taught me the value of delegating. She saw how much time I was spending doing day-to-day tasks and realized it was not a good use of my time. She came into my office one day, closed the door, and asked me to repeat after her these words, "I have people for that." She reminded me that I had a large department of capable and qualified people that I was not leveraging. I needed to recognize those talents and use them. I quickly learned how to do just that. Empowering them freed up my mind and my physical time to focus on other important work.

Delegation is the act of assigning authority to someone else to carry out a specific task or assignment. It requires the leader who is delegating the work to let go of responsibility while remaining accountable for the outcome.

Because it's easy to get pulled in a thousand different directions and because delegation and priority setting go hand in hand, here are a few best practices for priority setting:

1. Create a list.

2. Determine what is necessary vs. non-necessary.

3. It's ok to say "no" or "not right now" to more things.

4. Delegate important assignments to trusted leaders and staff. This gives them a sense of value while freeing you to focus on other things.

5. Breathe (take regular breaks).

6. Consider compromises you can make.

---

7. What are your most productive days of the week? Times of the day? (Weekends don't count.)

8. Tackle the most difficult task first.

9. Plan ahead whenever possible. For example, it's Friday. How can you set priorities for the next week? It can help you relax over the weekend.

10. Ask your assistant for help.

Delegation is most challenging if you haven't:

- Created an engaging work environment.
- Shared the business strategy with the team.
    - o Do they even know what is coming down the pike?
    - o Where are we going, how will we get there, why their role is important and how they can help.
- Recognized and rewarded acceptable and outstanding performance.
- Established (and followed) sound communication practices.

Delegation won't work without trust. If you don't trust an employee's capability, communication skills, or character, it will be difficult to consider delegating to them. Work through these trust issues to expand the circle of those you can delegate.

Your delegation matrix:

Based on work done by the Business Development Bank and Stephen Covey, let's start by evaluating whether you are using your free time productively.

	Urgent	**Not Urgent**
Important	**1)** We spend our time on: • Crises • Pressing problems • Deadline-driven projects, meetings, preparations (25%-30% of our time is spent here)	**2)** We spend our time on: • Preparation • Prevention • Values clarification • Planning • Relationship building • Needed relaxation • Empowerment (10%-15% of our time is spent here)
Not Important	**3)** We spend our time on: • Needless interruptions • Unnecessary reports • Unimportant meetings, phone calls, mail • Other people's minor issues	**4)** We spend our time on: • Trivia, busywork • Some phone calls • Time wasters • "Escape" activities • Irrelevant mail • Excessive TV watching • Excessive relaxation
	(55%-60% of our time is spent here)	

9 Delegation Techniques:

1. Take an objective look at your workload.
2. Determine where your contribution is most needed.
3. Identify the best people in the organization.
4. Train. Coach. Empower. Trust.
5. Share your business strategy with employees.
6. Develop repeatable processes.
7. Focus on results...without dead bodies.
8. Follow-up without micromanaging.
9. Encourage your direct reports to delegate.

Time Management Strategies:

- Create a daily plan.
- Assign time limits to complete each task.
- Use a calendar – stick to it.
- Desk or digital organizers are useful.
- Plot deadlines.
- Batch similar tasks together.
- Learn how to say "no," and when to say "no."
- Using an hourglass is a useful and fun way to keep yourself, and others focused and more time conscious.
- Block as many distractions as possible; ask others for help.
- Prioritize each day and each week.
- Use calendar buffers to give yourself a break before and after meetings.

Application:

A

Considering the Productivity Chart above, what are some ways you can reduce the amount of time you spend in Quadrants 1, 3 and 4 and redirect the time to Quadrant 2?

B

To what extent can you delegate the work that fits Quadrants 1, 3 and 4?

C

Next, ask yourself why haven't you delegated this work? Is it that you can't or that you won't?

Xiao rose through the company ranks and was known for his ingenious attention to detail and ability to get things done against all odds. As a jack-of-all-trades, he worked 100-hour weeks to make sure his department ran efficiently and effectively. Prior to his recent promotion to CEO, he had constantly texted each manager 24/7, asking them for hourly updates on the company's most important initiatives. However, with new responsibilities for developing strategy, leading Board Meetings, and traveling more extensively, he soon realized that his 100-hour work weeks were no longer feasible, and he would have to start delegating, but he was not sure where to start. Xiao's options included:

A   Hiring an administrative assistant to keep track of his 24/7 texts to all employees involved in important projects.

B   Assembling his direct reports, asking them to take direct responsibility for completing corporate initiatives and reporting back to Xiao on a weekly basis.

C   Implementing a chat software like Slack and inviting himself into all corporate conversations.

What is the best response? See the Scenario Answer Key at the end of the Playbook.

Complete at least one of these before moving to the next practice. Complete all three for deeper impact:

Set Your Mind: What's really robbing you of your time? Who can you tap for delegation opportunities? What is your next step?

Memorize: What will you commit to memory about this practice?

Exercise: Walk through the application and scenario again before moving to the next practice.

REFLECTION

Which insights from this practice most resonated with you?

....

....

....

....

ACTION PLAN

This is a ☐ 30 ☐ 60 ☐ 90 ☐ 180-day plan.

Start with the Action	The observable measure?	Target Date	Accountability Partner
Example: Improve my critical thinking skills.	Make more logical connections between ideas by asking the questions that lead to useful and effective outcomes.	March 30, 20xx	C. Jones

6. YOUR **NETWORK** MATTERS.

Case Study

In one executive role, a junior employee called me and said, "Meet me in the stairwell. I have something to tell you." While this might make some of you reading this cringe, it made me curious. So, to the stairwell I went to meet with this trusted employee. While it turned out not to be the sort of deep-throat information that my imagination had desired, it was very compelling, and I rightfully chose to do nothing with it. The insights proved to be true, and despite my desire to refrain from being used or manipulated, I learned how valuable it was for me to be able to maintain networks at all levels in the organization.

Achieving an executive advantage means you're able to see the company from multiple points of view. Being able to cultivate relationships at all levels in an organization while also being able to communicate in the same manner is crucial.

This doesn't come easily. We know our functional areas and serving as subject matter experts often takes us into a type of bias that makes it difficult to see others' points of view. To overcome this dilemma, leaders must take it upon themselves to create a broad network of insiders and outsiders who can offer multiple views of a given situation, allowing you to shape a well-rounded perspective that informs your thinking and covers your blind spots.

There are three types of networks to develop: internal, external, and a personal board of directors.

Internal networking is oft overlooked and downplayed; however, executives who've built strong internal networks will tell you it can make a difference in your effectiveness and your longevity within an organization. Consider it as having an ear to the ground and a pulse check on what is happening within the organization, as I did in the opening case.

External networking is the communication process that involves interacting with and engaging others to exchange information for the purposes of developing professional or social relationships that lead to:

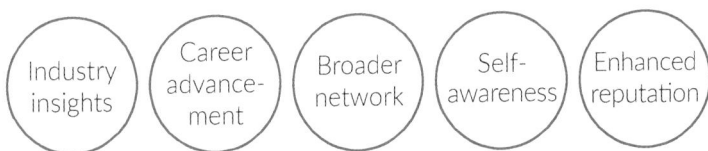

Industry insights • Career advance-ment • Broader network • Self-awareness • Enhanced reputation

This third network I call your personal board of directors. Executive strategists must be able to understand various points of view, not just their own, and have trusted individuals you can tap to exchange ideas and insights beyond a surface level.

For every department in the organization, as you move up, you'll want to make sure you have a broad enough network of people who reflect those departments. For example - senior-level individuals who head up HR, Communications, Technology, Public Relations, Operations, Marketing, and Finance departments. This is not to suggest you gather them as a group. On the contrary, these are individuals whose talents you can tap individually.

Expanding your network should be a strategic exercise:

- Evaluate whom you have in your network and who is missing.
- Examine your relationship with those in your network at the executive level.
- Establish a plan for filling the gap (volunteering, meet-ups, mixers, happy hours, etc.).
- Explore building new diverse relationships.
- Expand your network through intentional peer relationship-building efforts.

> *Networking is not about just connecting people.*
> *It's about connecting people with people, people with*
> *ideas, and people with opportunities.*

— Michele Jennae

Application:

You can't know everything. If you were to build a personal board of directors as described above, would you be able to do so quickly and easily? If not, what must change?

If networking is one of the keys to innovation and industry insights, to what extent would your current network support this?

Which of these areas are the most useful for your networking building strategy: LinkedIn, association membership, chapter volunteer role, board service, etc.?

Rosalind had a feeling that the Board's recent announcement to acquire their competitor fell like a thud within the company, and she was not sure what the fallout would be. It was important that she immediately address any doubts employees had before they posted on social media with comments about the acquisition. Having formal meetings wouldn't get her the information she needed to make quick moves, so she knew she'd need to get insights from her network to get a true perspective of how people felt. To get an accurate feel for company sentiment, Rosalind should:

A Send out a company-wide survey to all employees to measure their satisfaction with the news.

B Schedule formal meetings with key staff members to understand how their departments were adjusting to the news.

C Casually ask a few questions of trusted employees she met in the hallway at work and text a few who worked from home for a quick reply.

What is the best response? See the Scenario Answer Key at the end of the Playbook.

Complete at least one of these before moving to the next practice. Complete all three for deeper impact:

Set Your Mind: What is your level of satisfaction with your various networks? What changes or enhancements need to be made? Why? What will you do?

Memorize: What will you commit to memory about this practice?

Exercise: Walk through the application and scenario again before moving to the next practice.

REFLECTION

Which insights from this practice most resonated with you?

....

....

....

....

ACTION PLAN

This is a ☐ 30 ☐ 60 ☐ 90 ☐ 180-day plan.

Start with the Action	The observable measure?	Target Date	Accountability Partner
Example: *Improve my critical thinking skills.*	*Make more logical connections between ideas by asking the questions that lead to useful and effective outcomes.*	*March 30, 20xx*	*C. Jones*

PHASE 3:
LEADING THE ORGANIZATION

1. THE **CULTURE** MATTERS.

While culture is a complex approach to doing business, when you get right down to it, culture is simply "how you do things." But changing the culture requires more work than changing how you do things. Corporate culture plays a major role in job satisfaction, security, and your ability to attract and retain top talent. Fortunately, every individual you employ can have a powerful impact on your workplace. To create an environment where everyone can feel valued and appreciated, you must be in a constant state of self-examination of these aspects of culture:

You've heard it said that "change is inevitable, but growth is optional," and today's leaders realize that leadership is more challenging than ever. Today's leaders must learn how to embrace a new way of being and of leading themselves, their teams, and their organizations. If not, the culture will destroy your strategic efforts and your desires to achieve a competitive advantage.

To what extent are you evaluating your culture on a regular basis?

Make sure culture conversations are embedded in the organization's DNA.

The process of change can be very frustrating when it comes to culture shifts in organizations. Pressures from those on all sides of the organizational structure can dampen your efforts with their demands for immediate and sustained improvements.

For any change effort to take shape, here are some critical factors, just a few among many:

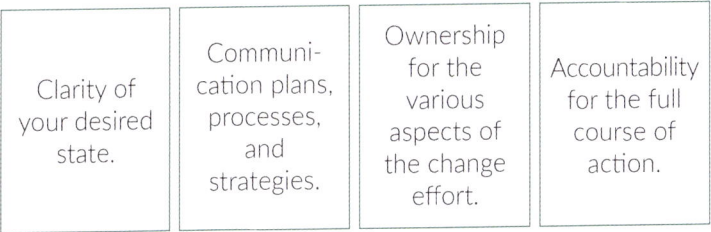

Clarity of your desired state.	Communi-cation plans, processes, and strategies.	Ownership for the various aspects of the change effort.	Accountability for the full course of action.

Accounting for each of these factors, however, is not enough because even when the landscape changes, the policies and procedures have been adopted, and the organization is more diverse and equitable, true inclusion will not come until you correct the effects of this one word:

MONOCULTURE

Your organization's culture is reinforced in the language used, how meetings are held, communication practices, human resource policies and systems, values that are reinforced, and other business traditions. When these norms are shaped by one dominant and prevailing culture, monocultural influences result.

Historically, in the U.S., many organizations' policies, laws, etc., have been shaped by white men. This worked when business was primarily run under their influence; however, business is now much more diverse. The laws, rules, regulations, structures, and approaches to business, while historically informative and possibly even useful, may no longer be as effective because it doesn't readily embrace the diverse perspectives of others. Others who have different needs, communication styles, work styles, decision processes, experiences, knowledge, and different views of change will find it challenging to navigate such a one-sided and outdated approach to work. This limits the organization's ability to obtain and maintain a competitive advantage, one enjoyed by organizations that are more diverse and inclusive. The reason this is important is because even during change, the monoculture is actively being preserved; everything that shaped the monoculture is embedded in the fabric of the organization and influences how we think and, therefore, how we behave. It doesn't mean that everyone in an organization believes and acts in the same way; it means we have accepted that way of being as the standard. If it goes unrecognized and unchallenged, it remains influential.

When you hit a monocultural wall, change efforts fail because while there is compliance, there is no connection, and therefore, accountability for changed behaviors becomes difficult. So, we change policies, modify procedures, and hire more diverse talent, yet goals are not being realized, and you can't figure out why there's still dissatisfaction.

To begin a shift from this ingrained influence, organizations must identify and hold themselves accountable for new practices that include:

- Speaking up when aggressive and passive-aggressive behaviors lead to others being excluded.
- Seeking to understand multicultural views in decision-making processes.
- A willingness to change your mind.
- Bridging low and high-context communication practices.
- Addressing and resolving misunderstandings while righting wrongs.
- Refraining from and calling out subversive behaviors that undermine change efforts.
- Adopting decision-making matrices and models that help push through the rigidity of extant systems.

Application:

Questions that can ensure you're exploring culture shifts include:

1. How has the culture changed in the past 6-12 months?
2. How does the culture need to change?
3. What's the desired culture now?
4. What are the behaviors that support this?
5. What's the link to our purpose?
6. What are the systems that will ensure accountability for these changes?

To understand more about cultural communication, I recommend *The Culture Map*, a book by Erin Meyer - a wonderful resource to help you understand the context of communication and related practices.

Scenario

Like many firms, Company X was having a hard time attracting and retaining young talent. Ricardo had recently stepped into the role of CEO as an outsider, finding that old norms and behaviors from their 50+ year history held little interest for younger candidates who search for value-based firms they can trust. HR had worked tirelessly to implement diversity, equity, and inclusion (DEI) policies that no one seemed to believe in or practice. Faced with the responsibility of leading the company into a new era while still keeping the lights on would be a challenge, as would aligning the culture with the needs of a younger generation. One of the first steps Ricardo should take should be:

A Force all department leaders to receive training on new HR policies.

B Survey the present culture, present a vision of what a cohesive, diverse culture looks like, and consistently share the vision across the company while adopting a change management strategy to realize the new vision.

C Wait for six months to see if the culture changes but ask HR to work harder at recruiting.

What is the best response? See the Scenario Answer Key at the end of the Playbook.

Complete at least one of these before moving to the next practice. Complete all three for deeper impact:

Set Your Mind: What role are you playing in either preserving and protecting the monoculture or in shifting it? What will you do now?

Memorize: What will you commit to memory about this practice?

Exercise: Explore culture shifts by walking through the application and reviewing the scenario above before moving to the next practice.

REFLECTION

Which insights from this practice most resonated with you?

....

....

....

....

ACTION PLAN

This is a ☐ 30 ☐ 60 ☐ 90 ☐ 180-day plan.

Start with the Action	The observable measure?	Target Date	Accountability Partner
Example: *Improve my critical thinking skills.*	*Make more logical connections between ideas by asking the questions that lead to useful and effective outcomes.*	*March 30, 20xx*	*C. Jones*

2. THE **DECISIONS** YOU MAKE MATTER.

Case Study

At 11 years old, Warren Buffett dove into the world of high finance by buying three shares of Cities Service that he later sold. He immediately regretted the decision as the numbers for Cities Service soared. Buffett learned his lessons about decision-making earlier than most, paving the way for the copious critical real-world decisions he was going to make.

Decision-making biases are cognitive biases that distort and disrupt our ability to objectively contemplate an issue by introducing influences into the decision-making process that are distinct from the decision itself. Usually, we are unaware of the biases that can affect our judgment.

Why?

- We see the world from our position(s).

- We perceive and express ourselves through our unique filters.

- We move towards our needs and motivations.

- We experience our world through our specific focus.

- Our ability to work through our biases begins with understanding our unique positions, filters, needs, and focus and how these affect others.

Had Mr. Buffet not recognized he'd made a bad decision (hindsight), learned from the bad decision (insight), and prepared for future decisions with the knowledge gained (foresight), he might not be the billionaire we know today. Making better decisions means we have to recognize roadblocks in these three (hindsight, insight, and foresight) areas. These roadblocks are traditionally referred to as Decision-Making Biases and include:

⊘ Confirmation bias:

This bias occurs when decision-makers seek out evidence that confirms their previously held beliefs while diminishing or discounting the impact of evidence that supports differing conclusions.

⚓ Anchoring:

This bias is the overreliance on an initial experience or single piece of information to make subsequent judgments. Once an anchor is set, other decisions are influenced by that anchor, which can limit one's ability to accurately interpret new, potentially relevant information.

◌ Halo effect:

This is an observer's overall impression of a person, product, brand, or company, and it influences the observer's thoughts and feelings about that entity's overall character or properties. For example, it is the perception that if someone does well in a certain area, they will automatically perform well at something else regardless of whether those tasks are related.

♔ Overconfidence bias:

This type of bias occurs when a person overestimates the reliability of their judgments. This can include the certainty one feels in their own ability, performance, level of control, or chance of success.

Before deciding, reflect on prior decisions (hindsight). Where have you often gone astray? Then, to gain insight or a deep understanding of the decision you face, and to prepare for a better decision, work through a pre-decision framework by answering some of the questions below to root out some of your decision-making biases:

- Should someone else who has the time to complete the entire picture make this decision?
- Does this decision have to be made by me or at this level? Can this decision be made closer to the front lines?
- Do I have a broad enough perspective to make and defend this decision?

- What might trigger an inappropriate response or decision?
- What are my biases (my preconceived notions) about this decision? What values or beliefs might influence my decision?
- Who can offer advice and feedback as to whether my thinking might be incomplete or if I've overlooked something important?

Source: Adapted from HBR: Root Out Bias from your Decision-making Process

Following a decision, you'll want to evaluate the effectiveness of that decision:

☐ Did the decision lead to intended outcomes?

☐ What were the strengths of the decision?

☐ What weaknesses were revealed because of the decision?

☐ What opportunities surfaced?

☐ What threats did we encounter (or do we anticipate) as a result of this decision?

☐ How did we remedy or mitigate the threat?

☐ What will we do unique, better, or differently than before if faced with a similar decision?

☐ Did the benefit of the decision outweigh the cost?

☐ What else?

Do you run through this process for each decision? Well, if you're trying to improve cognitive abilities, the answer is yes until you and others throughout the organization are practicing evaluative processes.

"

The world as we have created it is a process of our thinking. It cannot be changed without changing our thinking.

— Albert Einstein

"

Application:

Steps for Effective Decision Making:

1. Get a clear understanding of the situation that requires a decision.
2. Secondly, determine the exact decision to be made.
3. Assemble the relevant facts and related data.
4. Weigh the pros and cons against your goals.
5. Re-evaluate and discuss other options not already examined.
6. Determine the measures that indicate you've made a good decision.
7. Open discussion.
8. Make the decision.

Recover quickly from a bad decision by taking full responsibility and:

1. Acknowledge your emotions but don't let them consume you.
2. Focus on the present while being future-focused.
3. Respond quickly.
4. Identify a remedy (short/long-term).
5. Extract learning lessons for knowledge management.
6. Share learning lessons more broadly.

Scenario

The Board of Directors hired Samantha as CEO based on her ability to generate revenue and connect with customers. She had impeccable experience in customer success, building winning sales teams, and engaging staff members around strategic goals. Samantha soon learned that her success in the service sector would have little to do with leading a manufacturing company. Knowing almost nothing about raw materials, logistics, or transportation, Samantha was soon over her head in challenging issues, especially as supply chain problems put a stranglehold on the company's ability to deliver to customers.

Samantha's first inclination was to "wing it," but she soon discovered that her lack of manufacturing experience limited her decision-making ability. Samantha wanted to redeem her reputation and career and considered the following actions.

A Admit her inexperience, resign, and seek a more suitable industry role.

B Call in a consultant to provide advice about solving supply chain issues.

C Admit her inexperience and reach out to leaders in the company's manufacturing and logistics departments to collaborate on immediate customer solutions while building a long-term plan.

What is the best response? See the Scenario Answer Key at the end of the Playbook.

Complete at least one of these before moving to the next practice. Complete all three for deeper impact:

Set Your Mind: Assess your decision-making capabilities. What's coming to mind? What shifts will you set your mind to practice?

Memorize: What will you commit to memory about this practice?

Exercise: Before moving to the next practice, apply the strategy above to a decision you need to make or a decision that didn't turn out well. What did you learn?

REFLECTION

Which insights from this practice most resonated with you?

....

....

....

....

ACTION PLAN

This is a ☐ 30 ☐ 60 ☐ 90 ☐ 180-day plan.

Start with the Action	The observable measure?	Target Date	Accountability Partner
Example: *Improve my critical thinking skills.*	*Make more logical connections between ideas by asking the questions that lead to useful and effective outcomes.*	*March 30, 20xx*	*C. Jones*

3. YOUR **MEETINGS** MATTER.

Case Study

I recall working in one organization that leaders and staff termed as having a "high meeting culture." This means that every decision that needed to be made had to pass through some meeting. The ability and accountability for making decisions within the scope of one's leadership authority were all but non-existent. Even the CEO would run thoughts, decisions, ideas, and topics through a committee before vetting them further and acting. This was the least effective and least efficient way to conduct business. It was a sign that while individuals were awarded authority, no one wanted to take accountability for moving work forward, especially if there was the potential for mistakes.

Hint: If you have a lot of meetings where decisions are made by committee, it's likely a sign that the organization lacks accountability. It also signals the fear of risk-taking by those in leadership. Risk-averse organizations are the least innovative and lack the capacity for change. Therefore, if you seek a competitive advantage, you'll need to find a way to make better decisions faster and with fewer meetings. But if you must have a meeting, keep it short, to 30 minutes or less, and start making decisions without convening a meeting. Here are the six meetings every executive must have:

- Budget/Planning Meeting
- Strategic Planning (first team/second team)
- Executive Team Meetings
- Individual Direct Report Meetings
- Self-Reflection Meetings (yes, a meeting with yourself)
- Board/Governance Meetings

Effective meetings only occur when you have a clear purpose that includes making, ratifying, or communicating a decision or engaging in idea/information sharing. If you're going to have a meeting, here are some meeting practices to keep in mind:

- Start and end on time.
- Have an organized agenda.
- Effectively bring the discussion to a close and call for decisions when needed.
- Expectations, roles, and objectives of the meeting are clearly defined and understood.
- Have established ground rules and follow them.
- Keep the experience positive, work through conflict, and keep the momentum going.
- Decisions are documented and communicated.
- White space is built into the meeting to encourage broader communication of thoughts and ideas.

Too many meetings could be a sign that leaders and staff are not empowered or accountable for making decisions. This could be due to poor decision quality, the lack of delegation, an understanding of how to make quality decisions, and/or culture where groupthink is baked in the DNA.

Application:

In addition to the above tips, and to ensure you promote inclusion, here are some insights to reinforce inclusive meetings:

- Require diverse talent involvement in meetings.
- Become the role model for inclusive behaviors.
- Send meeting information in advance to promote engagement.
- Deal effectively and swiftly with dominating and/or negative personalities.
- Ensure all voices are heard - within and outside of the meeting.
- Mediate and facilitate - keep track of who's talking - and who's not. Exhibit zero tolerance for interruptions. Prevent anyone from dominating or derailing discussions.
- Follow-up after the meeting for insights and feedback.

Now go have better and fewer meetings.

Scenario

It seemed that Leo, the COO, was permanently attached to his iPad. His staff joked that no one knew the color of his eyes because Leo was constantly looking at his devices. Leo believed that technology helped him to multitask during meetings, but his actions forced his team to make decisions without his input. Leo did not see his actions as a problem. After all, his team seemed to get things done - wasn't that the point?

Jenice, VP of HR, approached Leo in the parking lot, demanding that he remove his earbuds. "In the last week, half of your team has submitted department transfer requests, and three more people resigned today. All of them reported that you don't listen, don't care, and don't get anything done in meetings. Don't you think it's time to 'unplug'?"

Based on this information, Leo should:

A Pause and listen to more of what Jenice says about his iPad being a distraction during meetings, including how his actions interfere with team engagement and decision-making.

B Begrudgingly commit to watching a webinar on "active listening" and "how to run better meetings."

C Make his assistant replace him in team meetings to prevent further complaints, having her email Leo a summary of team meeting notes.

What is the best response? See the Scenario Answer Key at the end of the Playbook.

Complete at least one of these before moving to the next practice. Complete all three for deeper impact:

Set Your Mind: Which of the meeting practices do you chronically overlook? What changes will you set your mind to make?

Memorize: What will you commit to memory about this practice?

Exercise: Write out a new meeting agenda you'll begin to adopt and do so before moving to the next practice.

REFLECTION

Which insights from this practice most resonated with you?

....

....

....

....

ACTION PLAN

This is a ☐ 30 ☐ 60 ☐ 90 ☐ 180-day plan.

Start with the Action	The observable measure?	Target Date	Accountability Partner
Example: *Improve my critical thinking skills.*	*Make more logical connections between ideas by asking the questions that lead to useful and effective outcomes.*	*March 30, 20xx*	*C. Jones*

4. **PRACTICE** LEADERSHIP MATTERS.

Case Study

One of my executive coaching clients said to me, "Pam, I want what's in your brain; I want to be able to know what you know and do what you do." What they were really saying is, "I admire the depth of your knowledge." It's a simple formula that is not always easy to follow: Identify a personal goal. Read, meditate, and practice. While some things are caught (passive adoption of new knowledge, skills, and abilities) and others are taught (the acquisition of new behaviors as the result of more deliberate work), to achieve executive advantage and build a distinctive brand, you'll need to be much more intentional. The best leaders and executives get to be the best through knowledge acquisition, management, and practice. What goals do you have? How will achieving an executive advantage get you there? What is the gap between what you know and what you need to know? What new behaviors will you adopt through practice?

The difference between the characteristics and the practices of executives with advantage is that skills are behaviors that can be practiced and developed over time and lead to an intended outcome or impact. However, not every behavior is a skill. For example, you can tell a story in such a way that the premise is either quickly understood or easily lost. To tell a story in which the premise, or intended impact, is received by the listener means you have developed that behavior in such a way that you are now skilled.

As I consider the executives I get to work with, I've identified these seven practices that make them impactful leaders.

(A) They manage their non-verbal communication.

The diversity of the workforce demands that its leaders and executives communicate effectively with people who have different communication needs, from the introvert and the extrovert to those who are more implicit than explicit communicators. These are not the same; they are different. Introversion has to do with how the energy for the engagement is experienced and therefore is internally focused, while implicit refers to how communication is expressed, received, and understood.

Practice

Be more explicit as a communicator and watch your facial expressions and body language. We're always communicating; just recognize what messages you want to send and use your body to communicate it effectively. Intentionality in communication is key.

(B) They are adaptable and flexible.

Flexibility is a short-term adjustment, while adaptability is a long-term change. Flexibility is often easy to adopt, while adaptability may be more difficult and require significant adjustment. For example, working remotely for a month (flexibility) vs. working remotely permanently (adaptability).

Practice

Be more flexible and adaptable by looking for ways to challenge your thinking. Look for change opportunities. Change your route to/from work. Look for better ways of doing the work. Apply various models to approach decisions or other ways of managing projects.

(C) They build relationships.

Find new people to know at different business levels and in different functions. Coffee shops and happy hour are the golf course of old. While quite a bit of business may still be conducted on the course, those who have family obligations have found other ways to connect informally. While it might cause you to pay the sitter an extra hour or get up early for a coffee meeting, the resulting relationship currency could be well worth the investment of time.

Practice

Get to know people by inviting one new person to lunch or coffee per week. Look for people who are at different levels in the organization, outside of the organization, and in different roles. Look for opportunities to serve on boards or volunteer on community projects and committees to expand your circle of influence. Perhaps there is someone who comments on your social media posts or who is active on social media whom you could share a virtual cup of coffee with? The goal is to expand your circle of influence. You'll be amazed and pleased by the value and volume of information and ideas that are embraced and exchanged.

(D) They read the room.

Not only must leaders be self-aware, but they must also be "other" aware. Many people communicate explicitly. However, the longer the team is together, the more implicit their communication styles become, shifting from more vocal to being more expressive in body language, position, and presence. Individuals who are new to a team often experience this as a "cold shoulder" feeling because they aren't yet aware of the implicit language of the team.

Practice

Observe and listen to what is and what is not being said in the meeting. Then compare it to what is being said outside of the meeting. What did others notice that you may have missed? Use this information to guide your interpretations of what is being communicated and your interactions within the meeting. This will help you learn how to quickly adjust your communication to fit what is needed in the moment, rather than push a previously established agenda and miss an opportunity to connect in more meaningful ways.

(E) They know how and when to speak up.

This is one of the biggest challenges yet one of the most critical responsibilities of a senior executive. Some refuse to speak up because of a culture of fear. Others simply don't do it well or don't know how to do so. Regardless of the reason for not speaking up, this responsibility distinguishes those who are attached to the organization's performance from those who are attached to their own performance. At the executive level, you'll not only need to learn how to speak up respectfully but practice doing so, especially to advocate for the vision, the purpose, and the advancement of the organization's culture. It's one of the most important and uncomfortable responsibilities of being an executive and leader and is at the very foundation of change. *Sidenote: If you're not afraid to speak up, are you one of the ones making it difficult for others to do so?*

Practice

Recognize the feelings that prevent you from speaking up. What's happening in you and in the room? What is the cause for which you feel the need to speak? Then practice your speaking up phrase. For me, I'd start the sentence with something like, "Following on to what Karen said, what if we think about it this way...." Then, get in the habit of asking powerful questions in addition to speaking up with your ideas. Often asking a powerful, thought-provoking question such as, "How will this impact our most loyal customers?" or "What are our competing priorities?" will open the floor for deeper discussion and for others to speak up. When others are able to join in, you've taken the focus off of yourself and put it back where it belongs, on the achievement of the organization's competitive advantage.

(F) They are life-long learners.

I have one CEO client that I secretly refer to as "the professor" because he's always sharing knowledge. I know that if I don't carry a pen and paper, I'm going to miss some nugget of insight and information he's going to share. He is the epitome of a life-long learner. We can't take our knowledge, skills, and abilities for granted by mistakenly believing what we know is all there is to know. Your effectiveness is only as good as the most recently acquired information you're practicing. Now, what if that information is outdated? While I'm not suggesting the pursuit of an additional degree, I am suggesting you challenge yourself and others to acquire insights on the latest thinking in their fields and reason it out with one another at work so you can take advantage of their thinking. This is where innovation and creativity come into play.

Practice

Challenge everyone on the team and in the organization to identify exactly how they are going to remain relevant in their roles. What are they reading? Who are they networking with? What groups and associations have they joined? What meetings are they attending? FINALLY, how will they bring that curated information back to the organization? Once they do, you'll need to challenge the team to identify knowledge management strategies to retain the information shared.

(G) They share information and tell meaningful stories.

Leaders thrive on data, but data alone has little value; it needs context to be fully useful. Additionally, data often report what happened. If you're trying to sell an idea, then combine data with a few analytics and a story to convey greater meaning to the work. Start by determining the problem you face and if you need a measure of what happened (hindsight), to gain insight into what is happening now (analysis), to forecast a possible future (analytics), or all three? Next, you'll convey a story that relates to the goal. If the goal is to understand what happened, then tell that story, and use that story or related stories to inform the analysis and to paint a picture of a better future with your analytics.

Practice

Create talking points to support the information being shared. Next, connect the talking points to relevant stories that relate meaning and purpose to the information presented. For example,

MEASURE	**ANALYSIS**	**ANALYTICS**
We had three discrimination claims by three high-performing employees.	The resignation of these three employees over a 6-month period has hurt morale, engagement, productivity, and the reputation of the department. We also saw a decline in customer experience scores during this time.	Employee focus groups, a 360 assessment of the manager, stay and exit interviews allow us to predict the possibility of future churn in the department and to assess the capability of the management to make a turnaround.

WHAT'S THE STORY?

A bad story:

"We lost three employees who claim discrimination, but we're taking all the leaders through diversity training and settled with the employees."

A better story:

"The organization did not do an effective job of developing, promoting, and holding its manager accountable for creating an engaging and productive work environment. The turnover of these three individuals has cost the organization $2.5 million in lost productivity, including a dip in revenue and other costs related to this issue. To correct the effects of this situation and to prevent future occurrences throughout the organization, I recommend the following actions...."

Not only did you lay the groundwork through proper analysis of the situation, but you've built a strong case using realistic change and support for the ask. What would you recommend?

Scenario

Norman couldn't sleep, deciding to get up and go for a 4 a.m. run. Despite all the glowing analytics and reports that 95% of strategic initiatives were in the "green" zone of being completed, his gut told him something was wrong. How could the financials provide a glowing story, but employees tell a different tale - especially those vindictive glances and acerbic social media posts? He had to get to the bottom of the issue. He knew if his employees didn't trust his actions as CEO, the KPIs didn't mean a darn thing.

Norman knew that he needed to get to the root of the employee issues and needed to increase trust from the lowest to the highest ranks. Norman should:

A Announce an "open door" policy where any of the 250 employees could come talk to him at any time.

B Hire a firm to conduct an anonymous 360 survey on employee sentiment and leadership performance, followed by concrete action steps and a commitment to practice new behaviors.

C Tell his leadership team they need to fix it.

What is the best response? See the Scenario Answer Key at the end of the Playbook.

Application:

Is there another practice that should be on the list? Decide which one you'll build on and create an action plan below to make improvements. You're investing in training and development experiences, but are you getting the return on those investments? How do you know?

Complete at least one of these before moving to the next practice. Complete all three for deeper impact:

Set Your Mind: Consider practices A-G above. Which needs your most immediate attention? What will you commit to?

Memorize: What will you commit to memory about this practice?

Exercise: Walk through the application and scenario again before moving to the next practice.

REFLECTION

Which insights from this practice most resonated with you?

....

....

....

....

ACTION PLAN

This is a ☐ 30 ☐ 60 ☐ 90 ☐ 180-day plan.

Start with the Action	The observable measure?	Target Date	Accountability Partner
Example: Improve my critical thinking skills.	*Make more logical connections between ideas by asking the questions that lead to useful and effective outcomes.*	*March 30, 20xx*	*C. Jones*

5. FIRST TEAM LEADERSHIP MATTERS.

Case Study

Often when I work with executive teams, they want to know, "Are we the worse team you've ever seen?" and the answer is always 'no' because I can't account for their personal experience, but I can account for mine. If there were a contest, I'd say my own C-team experience is one of the worse hands down, and hence, why I do this work today. We put the D in dysfunction. The biggest mistake was that everyone was attached to their own performance instead of to the performance of the organization, and none of the CEOs that I experienced through that organization could figure out how to get the team to operate as one: to see that their job was to focus not so much on their individual performance but on the organization's performance.

The "First Team" is a sports term that defines the starters for a game such as football. It has been used in recent years to reflect the senior leaders of an organization like the CEO, CHRO, CFO, and COO. Similarly, just as second-string sports players represent those who can play the game if a first-team member is taken out of the game, it is also used to refer to those individuals who report to first-team leaders in an organization. If appropriately developed, second-team leaders should be able to act in place of those first-team leaders they report to.

Arguably, one of the biggest challenges facing the C-suite is how the First Team (and sometimes even the second team) works together. Each step on the way to the top calls for an adjustment in your approach to leadership. Unfortunately, many leaders never get this message because they remain too attached to their performance to see how their behavior is impacting and influencing the organization. They mistakenly believe that what got them to their senior level will keep them there, so they double down on historical behaviors that lead to frustration for the leader, peers, and for everyone around them.

Individuals who achieve C-seats must adopt improved ways of leading, and the first step is in understanding who **their team** really is. The first team does what is best for the organization, not just for their department. I explained it like this to one client:

"When the C-suite operates effectively as a first-team, they understand that when a position comes open, it belongs to the organization, not the department. Therefore, the team decides the best use of those resources, not the 'department head'."

This process does not occur overnight. A significant amount of cognitive dissonance occurs but is needful for the full effectiveness of the team. The results include better decisions, clarity of objectives, goal alignment, improved interpersonal relationships, better decision quality, and the achievement of goals.

Reading both Patrick Lencioni's **The Five Dysfunctions of a Team** and **Start with Why** by Simon Sinek, you can get a clear understanding of why it's vital for the senior-most leaders to fully comprehend and embrace their roles at the top. The reason we have leaders is to embrace this work, but leaders are human, and humans do err. As such, this team of individuals needs help from time to time because their humanness has caused them to err.

The High-Performance Team Leadership Model™ that we've designed provides a visual of how you can envision yourself and your leadership team and every level of the organization.

With this model, you can visualize why your level of thinking needs to shift from one level to the next. The higher you go, the bigger the view, and a more customized set of skills is required. What skills are needed of you at this time, and of those skills, which need to be polished or further developed in YOU?

HPT Leadership Model™

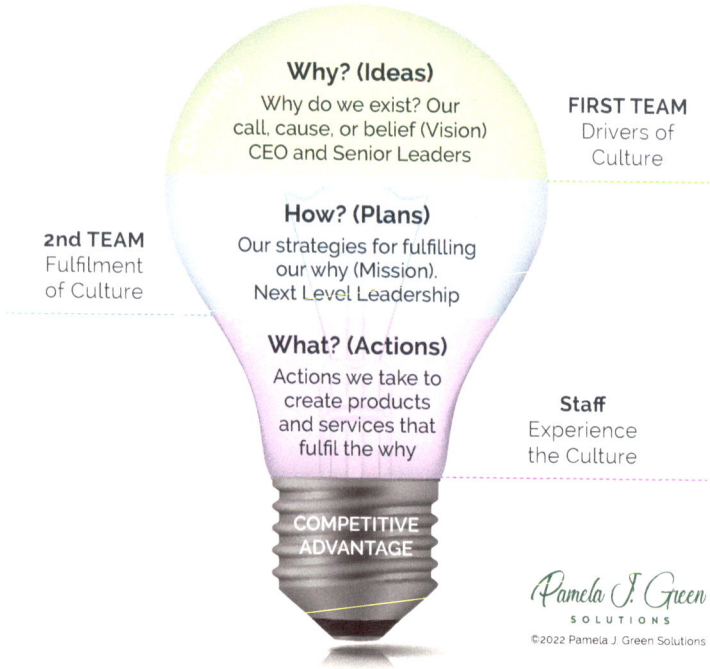

Why? (Ideas)
Why do we exist? Our
call, cause, or belief (Vision)
CEO and Senior Leaders

FIRST TEAM
Drivers of
Culture

2nd TEAM
Fulfilment
of Culture

How? (Plans)
Our strategies for fulfilling
our why (Mission).
Next Level Leadership

What? (Actions)
Actions we take to
create products
and services that
fulfil the why

Staff
Experience
the Culture

**COMPETITIVE
ADVANTAGE**

Pamela J. Green
S O L U T I O N S
©2022 Pamela J. Green Solutions

Unfortunately, becoming an effective executive is not as simple as picking up a book and thinking that you will be able to apply it to your organization; it would be like assuming that every headache could be remedied by acetaminophen. Every client and every company are as unique and different as your fingerprint, yet we still treat them the same. We go from one company to another thinking that the same set of talents, skills, and abilities will miraculously lead you and them to the advantage you were hired for. If it were this easy, we'd all be sharing space at the top, but we're not because it's not that easy. This playbook and other resources are useful to expand your knowledge and your thinking; however, they are not a blueprint for every situation because every situation is nuanced by the people in the situation.

Imagine being taken to a hospital full of physicians who haven't renewed their licenses in 10+ years. What type of experience do you think you'd have as one of their patients? Your advancement is your license to practice. Your credibility and the competitive advantage of the organization rest in your ability to not only practice but to become proficient. And once proficient, you can free your mind to focus on and develop additional skills such as the latest methods of management, communication, business strategy, and people engagement.

Application:

Can you assess where you are in the HPT model? Perhaps you're trying to determine if you're ready for or are performing well at the current level. The purpose of having management staff and management levels is to make sure the organization is making the best use of its resources. The various management levels are to close gaps and facilitate the achievement of goals. The level of knowledge and thinking gained from your education and your experience have a way of preparing you for the next level by permitting you to practice and become proficient where you are. Take this proficiency self-assessment to establish a baseline for your action plan.

A. I'm a novice and still learning.

B. I'm competent but practicing so I can improve.

C. I'm fully proficient. I do this well.

Level	A	B	C
Supervisory Skills			
Planning — Contribute to the development of goals by sharing insights gained from front-line interactions.			
Organizing — Structure the work in logical and practical ways that maximize resources.			

Level	A	B	C
Supervisory Skills continued			
Leading — Providing guidance and support to staff in their day-to-day responsibilities and activities such that they understand their role in helping the organization achieve its goals.			
Controlling — Monitors individual and team performance; upholds conduct, attitude, behavior, and performance standards.			
Middle Management Skills			
Planning — Contribute to the decision on which goals we'll pursue and provide guidance on strategies to adopt.			
Organizing — Facilitates the fulfillment of the mission by creating a shared meaning of the work, facilitating collaborative efforts, and promoting knowledge sharing and retention.			
Leading — Fostering the inclusion, development, and promotion of the talent and creating a pipeline of high-performance leaders.			
Controlling — Evaluates the degree to which team and department performance remain aligned to high-performance standards by measuring quality, customer experience, and productivity.			

Level	A	B	C
Senior/Executive Level Management Skills			
Planning — Decides upon the goals, strategies, and allocation of resources needed to attain organizational goals.			
Organizing — Determines the organizational structure best suited to promote the mission, engage and motivate the performance of talent to achieve business outcomes.			
Leading — Sponsoring and mentoring the succession and advancement of the talent; shapes and promotes only those who exhibit behaviors that reinforce and support your mission, vision, and values.			
Controlling — Assess and regulate the efficiency and effectiveness of teams and departments to achieve and maintain high-performance standards and outcomes.			

A. I'm a novice and still learning.

B. I'm competent but practicing so I can improve.

C. I'm fully proficient. I do this well.

It helps to have all the items in column C checked at each level to get a sense of your readiness to be proficient at the next level. If you have checked any items in column A or B, then work on those as you advance.

Juanita was elated after securing $10 million from an investor group. But then reality set in. Was her current executive staff ready to move into a new competitive realm? The 8-figure investment now meant everyone must be committed to long-term customer success, an ROI for her investors, and increasing employee engagement. Juanita found herself in new territory, understanding that company success depended on everyone's contribution.

The first thing Juanita should do is:

A Continue managing as always, hoping leaders will adjust accordingly to their new competitive status.

B Go on a well-deserved 3-week vacation, letting her leadership team run on autopilot until she returns. This would test their ability to lead in her absence and help her to see who emerges as a likely successor.

C Find a mentor and coach to help her and her team adapt to a cohesive, functional mindset shift, helping each person to identify and develop the new skills they would need to succeed in the new reality.

What is the best response? See the Scenario Answer Key at the end of the Playbook.

Complete at least one of these before moving to the next practice. Complete all three for deeper impact:

Set Your Mind: How does your thinking need to shift? Which leadership level (supervisor, middle management, or executive) are your behaviors more aligned with?

Memorize: What will you commit to memory about this practice?

Exercise: Walk through the application and scenario again before moving to the next practice.

REFLECTION

Which insights from this practice most resonated with you?

....

....

....

....

ACTION PLAN

This is a ☐ 30 ☐ 60 ☐ 90 ☐ 180-day plan.

Start with the Action	The observable measure?	Target Date	Accountability Partner
Example: Improve my critical thinking skills.	*Make more logical connections between ideas by asking the questions that lead to useful and effective outcomes.*	*March 30, 20xx*	*C. Jones*

PARTING THOUGHTS:

Leadership should be exhilarating and challenging. With so much in the world of business changing rapidly and the demand for agility, can you afford to stop learning, growing, and practicing new ways of leading? The lack of conceptual skills such as decision-making, communication, business analysis, critical thinking, and cognitive skills can put your brand and your organization in jeopardy. I realize it is impossible to know everything there is to know about leadership and to be a perfect leader. But I'm not after perfection. I'm after practice because practicing better ways of leading paves the way to progress. Do you want to make and sustain professional progress?

So, here's my charge to you:

A **Complete a skills inventory annually.** You can complete our leadership skills inventory adapted from Robert L. Katz's work by visiting the pamelajgreen.com website. Our tool is designed to help you gain insight into your technical, social, and conceptual leadership competencies. You can use it to conduct your leadership SWOT/TOWS discussed in Phase 2: Leading Others, 1. Leadership Styles Matter. Mind Tools also has a number of free online assessments.

B **Next, use your outcomes from the inventory to create a list of resources to close the gap.** Some people read books, others listen to them, some attend conferences and training events, and others like articles and micro-learning opportunities. Doing this will provide nourishment for your mind and enhance your cognitive abilities.

C **Finally, practice one new social or conceptual skill per quarter** - no less than two per year. Take your brand and your organization out of jeopardy by applying a new concept and teaching it to others.

By this time next year, I expect to hear how much you've developed as a leader and executive. Thank you for trusting me with your brand.

JOURNAL YOUR REFLECTIONS

Capture notes and insights as you work through this playbook.

SCENARIO
ANSWER KEY

1. Your Thinking Matters.

Scenario Answer: A - To remedy the inefficiencies, you brainstorm potential options, test solutions, and use the insights to decide how and when to move forward.

Leaders who focus on what matters most to themselves stop short of looking at the situation from a broader perspective. Being concerned with one's situation is how individual contributors think, not how globally minded leaders think. Listening to others who share the same perspective is the brain's way of seeking confirmation and often keeps us at a standstill. Adopt critical thinking processes so that you and others explore the possibility for improved efficiencies and effectiveness, which is the cornerstone of high-performing organizations. Options B and C do not respond to the sense of urgency, nor do they reflect a leader who is developing responsive and nimble teams. These two options could lead to more of the same status quo.

2. Being Centered Matters.

Scenario Answer: B - You continue to perform at a high level and secure trusted advisors such as a coach, mentor, and therapist to help you work through the dilemma. This would help you make an informed rather than an emotional decision.

Being centered means you've given yourself the space to think through situations critically. It also means you leverage resources to help you process situations if you know you are too emotionally connected to think clearly. Sometimes resources are licensed professionals, and sometimes peers or other leaders can help you think through the situation. Going to the board, as referenced in

Option C, is extremely risky because boards tend to hold allegiance to the CEO and going to the board chair could backfire. Option A is the nuclear option; the one you take when you're out of all other options. However, Option A could be more viable if you have saved funds to cover at least a year or two of your expenses, but not a first option. I try to get leaders to work through dilemmas and leave the nuclear option as an absolute last resort. There is often much to be benefited from the struggles of leadership.

3. Your Behavior Matters.

Scenario Answer: C - Take time to communicate a clear and thoughtful plan for the future that guides all employees on what to expect from her as a leader, providing frequent updates and KPIs on the leadership team's success in reaching goals.

Using referent and expert power, Lyndsey can step into her new role as CEO, helping all employees to adjust to her leadership dynamic. By communicating her progress, along with clear measurements, she can work collaboratively with her team and reflect on the success of her plan. Option A will likely lead to turnover, perhaps of her knowledge workers, and result in disgruntled employees who may quietly quit without actually leaving the company, hurting productivity and morale. Option B panders to the tenured employees as a way of buying their loyalty and support, which will expose her vulnerabilities and most certainly backfire. Once she is exposed, recovery will be a challenge. A better approach to engagement and leadership is found in Option C.

4. Accountability Matters.

Scenario Answer: B - Consult with the product development team about XYZ's news and define new expectations for product delivery, sharing the potential revenue and market share consequences for sticking to the original 6-month timeline.

Changes happen, requiring leaders to redefine expectations for all parties. By clarifying the consequences of sticking to the original plan, Aran can work with the product team to develop alternatives so that all parties have clear expectations, remain accountable, and understand the consequences. ABC has a high standard of excellence and speeding up a timeline without regard to quality will end in disastrous results. It also allows them to observe the first-to-market hiccups that XYZ will experience and consider any needed adjustments to their product. Option A is reckless and signals a leader with extreme egocentric behaviors. Option C is another reckless leadership behavior, this time, it jeopardizes quality and could ultimately risk its reputation and customer loyalty.

5. Coaching Matters.

Scenario Answer: B - Keep the appointment, but ask the current coach about their coaching philosophy, success with previous employees in Bella's situation, and expectations for the future.

The circumstances of moving to a new country, starting a new job, and being assigned a new coach are bound to create problems. Stopping to evaluate the situation and discuss the coach's credentials and philosophies will help Bella decide if they can continue working together while also defining what she needs from a future coach. Option A offers no guarantee you'll identify a coach that has a better fit unless you first understand what exactly you need. Having an exploratory conversation with the current coach could inform your current and potential future coach relationships. Option C is a misuse of the sponsorship relationship. Sponsors aren't mentors; they are advocates. Once in the job, now it's important to identify mentors who can provide the type of advice Bella is looking for.

LEADING OTHERS

1. Leadership Styles Matter.

Scenario Answer: B - Evaluate how his autocratic, maverick style has both strengths and weaknesses that may be holding him back.

Gerald's "my way or the highway" approach can be both his strength and his weakness, especially if the executive team does not trust his approach. Taking time to do a SWOT and TOWS analysis, especially with the support of a coach, can help Gerald see where his approach is appropriate and how he can adapt to the needs of his new company. The operative word in Option A is "trust," and since Gerald hasn't built trust, this option will most certainly contribute to his failure to lead this company. Option C is the extreme opposite of his authoritarian style and can make others feel as if they are being set up to fail. It presents as "ok, fine, do it your way and see what happens." There must be a collaboration of styles and an adjustment of his approach that includes a focus on relationship and trust building if Gerald is to realize long-term success in this company.

2. Your Communication Matters.

Scenario Answer: A - Communicate the top five most important findings of his report while saving half of his presentation time to answer questions from Board Members and senior leadership.

Jules' detailed presentation style doesn't work for an audience who does not comprehend numbers like a financial expert, showing their disinterest through lack of engagement and glazed eyes. The Board needs to know the essential information first, what action steps should be considered, and understand the consequences of those actions. Make it simple for the audience to understand the most critical information and tell them what they need to do about it. In his book, ***Empowering Yourself, The Organizational Game Revealed***, Harvey Coleman asserts that performance is the smallest determinant of leadership success. Suggesting leaders focus on their exposure and image to be effective and influential leaders. In part, I might agree, and research supports that at the leadership level, there is less emphasis on your skills or technical abilities. However, outside the lines of this model is the need to emphasize your conceptual and social skills (see Executive Master at the front of this journal for a refresher on this). Therefore, PIE as a model alluded to in Option B, is only part of what is needed by Jules. Without an emphasis on his conceptual and social skills, improving his image may not be effective. Option C, like Option B, emphasizes another element of PIE – image - when the real issue is with Jules' communication approach. Fixing this could more quickly improve his image with his audience.

3. Conflict Leadership Matters.

Scenario Answer: B - Challenge each person to make a list of the top 10 best practices that work in each of their regions, including measured results, choose the best ideas, and then present a plan to the CEO.

Each person should expand upon the success stories of each other and present the best ideas to the CEO. When a company is in trouble, collaborating for the company's health instead of personal interests helps everyone. If Victoria and Oliver spend time with Options A or C, they are leaders unable to shift from their myopic technical expertise to the demand of mature leaders. Leaders who can approach their work more collaboratively and from a broader view of what is needed for the company - and not simply to fulfill their egotistical drive.

4. Collaboration Matters.

Scenario Answer: **A** - Sponsor a weekend retreat with all his Vice Presidents to brainstorm ideas for new products and services, hiring an outside professional facilitator to guide the discussions. At the end of the meeting, they would create a list of people responsible for putting these new ideas into action.

Collaboration is an amalgamation of inventive ideas and putting those ideas into action. The weekend retreat helps put peers at ease, offering a supportive environment for creation while assigning responsibilities and next steps. Answers B and C offer new ideas but no framework for putting those ideas into action. Notice that Solution A does not permanently resolve the issue with silos, which deserves a different strategy and calls for an intentional effort by senior leadership and middle management to address the issue.

5. Delegation Matters.

Scenario Answer: **B** - Assembling his direct reports, asking them to take direct responsibility for completing corporate initiatives and reporting back to Xiao weekly.

Delegating requires assigning projects to people who can be trusted, accountable, and provide results you can count on. Handling strategic initiatives is part of a direct report's essential job duties, and they should be counted on to provide information consistently. Option A doesn't necessarily mitigate the issue as the work needs to be delegated, not the tracking of texts. Option C feeds his addiction to work and could result in an organization of individuals who follow his leadership style, which precipitates a decline in engagement, morale, and productivity.

6. Your Network Matters.

Scenario Answer: C - Casually ask a few questions of trusted employees she met in the hallway at work and text a few who worked from home for a quick reply.

Networking, especially for sensitive information, is best kept to trusted people whom you know will give you an honest, unbiased answer. The more quickly you can get input, the faster you can get insight into the impact of important news. Option A may not yield the best insights because employees will likely respond in a way they deem most favorable to the leader and not reveal their true thoughts about the matter. Option B is another version of Option A, will likely lead to the same outcome and is more time-consuming.

LEADING THE ORGANIZATION

1. The Culture Matters.

Scenario Answer: B - Survey the present culture, present a vision of what a cohesive, diverse culture looks like and consistently share the vision across the company.

Typically, the culture changes following changes in practices, policies, and procedures. To create a path to a new culture, Ricardo needs to benchmark where the culture is now and create a vision of what it could be like. Communicating the vision helps engage current staff walking through a change management strategy, including attracting new talent. Training alone, Option A, is a waste of money and needs to be augmented by a commitment to practice new behaviors, sharing knowledge with others, mentoring, enhanced feedback, and a tie to outcomes in order to be effective. All these methods take time and should be incorporated into any change management plan. Also, training on policies does not equate to practice. Option C, well, let's just have a good laugh together with that one.

2. The Decisions You Make Matter.

Scenario Answer: C - Admit her inexperience and reach out to leaders in the company's manufacturing and logistics departments to collaborate on immediate customer solutions while building a long-term plan.

Like most CEOs, Samantha is encountering a new situation where she needs expert solutions from people who know the business and the issues. By engaging with leaders in her own company, she improves engagement, gets started on an immediate solution, and sets the stage for a long-term plan. A leader who repeatedly chooses Option A is looking for a way out, not an opportunity for their own growth and development. It's a sign that the leader might not be a lifelong learner, and if you move up and around, there is much to learn at every step. Don't run simply because it gets difficult. Ask yourself, what do I need to learn here? What conceptual or social skills are lacking? Do I need to know something, or is there someone on the team or in the organization who knows and can help? Option B is good for the consultant, but most companies don't know how to leverage consultants effectively (that's for the next book), so they pay a lot and don't get much in return. Besides, supply chain issues are just a part of the problem. Look within for the answers; most of the time, the solution is found there. Then hire experts from the outside to help you expedite your plan.

3. Your Meetings Matter.

Scenario Answer: A - Pause and listen to more of what Jenice has to say about his iPad being a distraction during meetings, including how his actions interfere with team engagement and decision-making.

Leo's behavior is distracting. His focus on his own job efficiency, instead of team collaboration, prevents his department from contributing to strategic decisions. Leaders must bring their "A" game, giving each meeting a purpose and outcome. People first, tech second. Option A has the greatest chance of leading to changed behaviors. Option B doesn't guarantee that Leo will behave differently. Option C is a trap that feels like delegation but is abdication instead. Less of Leo could result in....less of Leo.

4. Practice Leadership Matters.

Scenario Answer: B - Hire a firm to conduct an anonymous 360 survey on employee sentiment and leadership performance, followed by concrete action steps.

Norman is "reading the room" that something is wrong, despite the glowing financial facts. By hiring an independent firm to conduct an anonymous survey, they can help get to the root of the issue without inserting any bias that may come from a leadership-developed survey. Once key issues are identified, the company can communicate the results and provide a clear action plan for correction. This includes a plan for practicing new behaviors. With the concern for trust, Option A is a nice gesture but might not yield the honesty and insights he seeks. On the other hand, what if all 250 employees took Norman up on his offer? How would he manage the conversations and capture the feedback limiting as much bias as possible? Option C is a common practice that doesn't consider that the leaders might hold some of the same concerns as staff. If this is the case, what exactly would the leaders be "fixing?"

5. First Team Leadership Matters.

Scenario Answer: C - Find a mentor and coach to help her and her team adapt to a cohesive, functional mindset shift, helping each person identify and develop the new skills they would need to succeed in the new environment.

As the company rises to a new level of engagement, the leadership team must shift their thinking to an "us" mentality. A shift of this magnitude requires a concerted effort of development, where everyone puts the needs of the organization first, aligning goals with the needs of what is best for the whole. Learning and growing together will move them from dysfunction to distinction in a shorter period. Option A yields some winners and some losers. What if one of the losers has a domino effect on the organization? Option B offers no realistic solution.

SET YOUR
MIND

Set your mind ahead of time on the good outcomes you want for yourself and others, and repeat:

I am thankful for.....

(Believe that every experience can be used for your good.)

I will release.......

(Let go of negative experiences so they don't permanently imprint your thinking.)

I will change....

(Identify the needed change in your conduct, attitude, and behavior.)

I expect....

(Say what you expect for the outcome - out loud.)

I will act.

(Put what you believe to practice.)

HERE'S TO YOUR SUCCESS.

As top-rated executive coaches, we enjoy partnering with CEOs and their teams to transform cultures, boost executive excellence and guide you to mastery. Become a more effective executive and start working with Pam and her team today.

Follow our insights on Twitter
@pamelajgreen

Join our community of leaders at
www.pamelajgreen.com

Follow us on LinkedIn
www.linkedin.com/company/pamelajgreensolutions/

Ask questions at
customercare@pamelajgreen.com

Meet Pam and see her in action on YouTube
www.youtube.com/c/PamelaJGreen/videos

APSEA™ is a trademark of Pamela J. Green Solutions.

Brand Adjacencies™ is a trademark of Pamela J. Green Solutions.

High-Performance Team Leadership Model™ is a trademark of Pamela J. Green Solutions.

PAMELA J. GREEN,
MBA, SPHR, PCC

Voted one of DC's top 20 coaches; she is an international educator, executive coach, consultant, and researcher. As a leadership consultant, Mrs. Green supports global corporations, small businesses, non-profit organizations, leadership teams, and boards, developing strategies to achieve competitive advantage. Executives call on Pamela to fine-tune their competitive edge and shape their cultures to achieve breakthrough performance with their business strategies, leadership initiatives, and professional careers. In addition, Pam's approachable style as a facilitator and executive coach enables her to create a psychologically safe environment for her clients to make transformative and sustainable shifts in their conduct, attitude, and behavior.

www.ingramcontent.com/pod-product-compliance
Lightning Source LLC
Chambersburg PA
CBHW040243230326
41458CB00104B/6469